Microsoft

MOS 2016 Study Guide for Microsoft Excel Expert

Paul McFedries

Microsoft Office Specialist
Exam 77-728

MOS 2016 Study Guide for Microsoft Excel Expert

Published with the authorization of Microsoft Corporation by:
Pearson Education, Inc.

ISBN-13: 978-0-7356-9942-7
ISBN-10: 0-7356-9942-9

Library of Congress Control Number: 2016953074

1 16

For information about buying this title in bulk quantities, or for special sales opportunities (which may include electronic versions; custom cover designs; and content particular to your business, training goals, marketing focus, or branding interests), please contact our corporate sales department at corpsales@pearsoned.com or (800) 382-3419.

For government sales inquiries, please contact governmentsales@pearsoned.com.

For questions about sales outside the U.S., please contact intlcs@pearson.com.

Editor-in-Chief
Greg Wiegand

Senior Acquisitions Editor
Laura Norman

Senior Production Editor
Tracey Croom

Editorial Production
Online Training Solutions, Inc.
(OTSI)

Series Project Editor/
Copy Editor
Kathy Krause (OTSI)

Technical Editor
Joan Lambert (OTSI)

Compositor/Indexer
Susie Carr (OTSI)

Proofreader
Jaime Odell (OTSI)

Editorial Assistant
Cindy J. Teeters

Interior Designer
Joan Lambert (OTSI)

Cover Designer
Twist Creative • Seattle

Contents

What do you think of this book? We want to hear from you!

Microsoft is interested in hearing your feedback so we can improve our books and learning resources for you. To participate in a brief survey, please visit:

https://aka.ms/tellpress

What do you think of this book? We want to hear from you!

Microsoft is interested in hearing your feedback so we can improve our books and learning resources for you. To participate in a brief survey, please visit:

https://aka.ms/tellpress

Introduction

The Microsoft Office Specialist (MOS) certification program has been designed to validate your knowledge of and ability to use programs in the Microsoft Office 2016 suite of programs. This book has been designed to guide you in studying the types of tasks you are likely to be required to demonstrate in Exam 77-728, Excel 2016 Expert: Interpreting Data for Insights.

> **Exam Strategy** For information about the tasks you are likely to be required to demonstrate in the core Excel exam, Exam 77-727, Excel 2016: Core Data Analysis, Manipulation, and Presentation, see *MOS 2016 Study Guide for Microsoft Excel* by Joan Lambert (Microsoft Press, 2017).

Who this book is for

MOS 2016 Study Guide for Microsoft Excel Expert is designed for experienced computer users seeking Microsoft Office Specialist Expert certification in Excel 2016.

MOS exams for individual programs are practical rather than theoretical. You must demonstrate that you can complete certain tasks or projects rather than simply answer questions about program features. The successful MOS certification candidate will have at least six months of experience using all aspects of the program on a regular basis; for example, protecting a worksheet, applying conditional formatting rules, using a formula to look up a value, and building a PivotTable.

As a certification candidate, you probably have a lot of experience with the program you want to become certified in. Many of the procedures described in this book will be familiar to you; others might not be. Read through each study section and ensure that you are familiar with the procedures, concepts, and tools discussed. In some cases, images depict the tools you will use to perform procedures related to the skill set. Study the images and ensure that you are familiar with the options available for each tool.

How this book is organized

The exam coverage is divided into chapters representing broad skill sets that correlate to the functional groups covered by the exam. Each chapter is divided into sections addressing groups of related skills that correlate to the exam objectives. Each section includes review information, generic procedures, and practice tasks you can complete on your own while studying. You can use the provided practice files to work through the practice tasks, and the result files to check your work. You can practice the generic procedures in this book by using the practice files supplied or by using your own files.

Throughout this book, you will find Exam Strategy tips that present information about the scope of study that is necessary to ensure that you achieve mastery of a skill set and are successful in your certification effort.

Download the practice files

Before you can complete the practice tasks in this book, you need to copy the book's practice files and result files to your computer. Download the compressed (zipped) folder from the following page, and extract the files from it to a folder (such as your Documents folder) on your computer:

https://aka.ms/MOSExcelExpert2016/downloads

> **IMPORTANT** The Excel 2016 program is not available from this website. You should purchase and install that program before using this book.

You will save the completed versions of practice files that you modify while working through the practice tasks in this book. If you later want to repeat the practice tasks, you can download the original practice files again.

The following table lists the practice files provided for this book.

Folder and objective group	Practice files	Result files
MOSExcelExpert2016\Objective1 Manage workbook options and settings	ExcelExpert_1-1a.xlsx ExcelExpert_1-1b.xlsm ExcelExpert_1-2a.xlsx ExcelExpert_1-2b.xlsx ExcelExpert_1-2c.xlsx ExcelExpert_1-2d.xlsx	ExcelExpert_1-1a_results.xlsx ExcelExpert_1-1b_results.xlsm ExcelExpert_1-2a_results.xlsx ExcelExpert_1-2b_results.xlsx ExcelExpert_1-2c_results.xlsx ExcelExpert_1-2d_results.xlsx
MOSExcelExpert2016\Objective2 Apply custom data formats and layouts	ExcelExpert_2-1.xlsx ExcelExpert_2-2a.xlsx ExcelExpert_2-2b.xlsx ExcelExpert_2-2c.xlsx ExcelExpert_2-3.xlsx ExcelExpert_2-4.xlsx	ExcelExpert_2-1_results.xlsx ExcelExpert_2-2a_results.xlsx ExcelExpert_2-2b_results.xlsx ExcelExpert_2-2c_results.xlsx ExcelExpert_2-3_results.xlsx
MOSExcelExpert2016\Objective3 Create advanced formulas	ExcelExpert_3-1.xlsx ExcelExpert_3-2.xlsx ExcelExpert_3-3.xlsx ExcelExpert_3-4.xlsx ExcelExpert_3-4_CSV.csv ExcelExpert_3-4a.xlsx ExcelExpert_3-4b.xlsx ExcelExpert_3-4c.xlsx ExcelExpert_3-4d.xlsx ExcelExpert_3-4e.xlsx ExcelExpert_3-4f.xlsx ExcelExpert_3-5.xlsx ExcelExpert_3-6.xlsx	ExcelExpert_3-1_results.xlsx ExcelExpert_3-2_results.xlsx ExcelExpert_3-3_results.xlsx ExcelExpert_3-4_results.xlsx ExcelExpert_3-5_results.xlsx ExcelExpert_3-6_results.xlsx
MOSExcelExpert2016\Objective4 Create advanced charts and tables	ExcelExpert_4-1.xlsx ExcelExpert_4-2.xlsx ExcelExpert_4-3.xlsx	ExcelExpert_4-1_results.xlsx ExcelExpert_4-2_results.xlsx ExcelExpert_4-3_results.xlsx

Ebook edition

If you're reading the ebook edition of this book, you can do the following:

- Search the full text
- Print
- Copy and paste

You can purchase and download the ebook edition from the Microsoft Press Store at:

https://aka.ms/MOSExcelExpert2016/detail

Errata, updates, and book support

We've made every effort to ensure the accuracy of this book and its companion content. If you discover an error, please submit it to us through the link at:

https://aka.ms/MOSExcelExpert2016/errata

If you need to contact the Microsoft Press Book Support team, please send an email message to:

mspinput@microsoft.com

For help with Microsoft software and hardware, go to:

https://support.microsoft.com

We want to hear from you

At Microsoft Press, your satisfaction is our top priority, and your feedback our most valuable asset. Please tell us what you think of this book by completing the survey at:

https://aka.ms/tellpress

The survey is short, and we read every one of your comments and ideas. Thanks in advance for your input!

Stay in touch

Let's keep the conversation going! We're on Twitter at:

https://twitter.com/MicrosoftPress

Taking a Microsoft Office Specialist exam

Desktop computing proficiency is increasingly important in today's business world. When screening, hiring, and training employees, employers can feel reassured by relying on the objectivity and consistency of technology certification to ensure the competence of their workforce. As an employee or job seeker, you can use technology certification to prove that you already have the skills you need to succeed, saving current and future employers the time and expense of training you.

Microsoft Office Specialist certification

Microsoft Office Specialist certification is designed to assist students and information workers in validating their skills with Office programs. The following certification paths are available:

- A Microsoft Office Specialist (MOS) is an individual who has demonstrated proficiency by passing a certification exam in one or more Office programs, including Microsoft Word, Excel, PowerPoint, Outlook, or Access.

- A Microsoft Office Specialist Expert (MOS Expert) is an individual who has taken his or her knowledge of Office to the next level and has demonstrated by passing two certification exams that he or she has mastered the more advanced features of Word or Excel.

- A Microsoft Office Specialist Master (MOS Master) is an individual who has demonstrated a broader knowledge of Office skills by passing the Word and Word Expert exams, the Excel and Excel Expert exams, and the PowerPoint, Access, or Outlook exam.

Selecting a certification path

When deciding which certifications you would like to pursue, assess the following:

- The program and program version(s) with which you are familiar
- The length of time you have used the program and how frequently you use it

- Whether you have had formal or informal training in the use of that program

- Whether you use most or all of the available program features

- Whether you are considered a go-to resource by business associates, friends, and family members who have difficulty with the program

Candidates for MOS Expert and MOS Master certification are expected to successfully complete a wide range of standard business tasks. Successful candidates generally have six or more months of experience with the specific Office program, including either formal, instructor-led training or self-study using MOS-approved books, guides, or interactive computer-based materials.

Candidates for MOS Expert and MOS Master certification are expected to successfully complete more complex tasks that involve using the advanced functionality of the program. Successful candidates generally have at least six months, and might have several years, of experience with the programs, including formal, instructor-led training or self-study using MOS-approved materials.

Test-taking tips

Every MOS certification exam is developed from a set of exam skill standards (referred to as the *objective domain*) that are derived from studies of how the Office programs are used in the workplace. Because these skill standards dictate the scope of each exam, they provide critical information about how to prepare for certification. This book follows the structure of the published exam objectives.

See Also For more information about the book structure, see "How this book is organized" in the Introduction.

The MOS certification exams are performance based and require you to complete business-related tasks in the program for which you are seeking certification. For example, you might be presented with a document and told to insert and format additional document elements. Your score on the exam reflects how many of the requested tasks you complete within the allotted time.

Here is some helpful information about taking the exam:

- Keep track of the time. Your exam time does not officially begin until after you finish reading the instructions provided at the beginning of the exam. During the exam, the amount of time remaining is shown in the exam instruction window. You can't pause the exam after you start it.

- Pace yourself. At the beginning of the exam, you will receive information about the tasks that are included in the exam. During the exam, the number of completed and remaining tasks is shown in the exam instruction window.

- Read the exam instructions carefully before beginning. Follow all the instructions provided completely and accurately.

- If you have difficulty performing a task, you can restart it without affecting the result of any completed tasks, or you can skip the task and come back to it after you finish the other tasks on the exam.

- Enter requested information as it appears in the instructions, but without duplicating the formatting unless you are specifically instructed to do so. For example, the text and values you are asked to enter might appear in the instructions in bold and underlined text, but you should enter the information without applying these formats.

- Close all dialog boxes before proceeding to the next exam item unless you are specifically instructed not to do so.

- Don't close task panes before proceeding to the next exam item unless you are specifically instructed to do so.

- If you are asked to print a document, worksheet, chart, report, or slide, perform the task, but be aware that nothing will actually be printed.

- Don't worry about extra keystrokes or mouse clicks. Your work is scored based on its result, not on the method you use to achieve that result (unless a specific method is indicated in the instructions).

- If a computer problem occurs during the exam (for example, if the exam does not respond or the mouse no longer functions) or if a power outage occurs, contact a testing center administrator immediately. The administrator will restart the computer and return the exam to the point where the interruption occurred, with your score intact.

◇◇

Exam Strategy This book includes special tips for effectively studying for the Microsoft Office Specialist exams in Exam Strategy paragraphs such as this one.

◇◇

Certification benefits

At the conclusion of the exam, you will receive a score report, indicating whether you passed the exam. If your score meets or exceeds the passing standard (the minimum required score), you will be contacted by email by the Microsoft Certification Program team. The email message you receive will include your Microsoft Certification ID and links to online resources, including the Microsoft Certified Professional site. On this site, you can download or order a printed certificate, create a virtual business card, order an ID card, review and share your certification transcript, access the Logo Builder, and access other useful and interesting resources, including special offers from Microsoft and affiliated companies.

Depending on the level of certification you achieve, you will qualify to display one of three logos on your business card and other personal promotional materials. These logos attest to the fact that you are proficient in the applications or cross-application skills necessary to achieve the certification. Using the Logo Builder, you can create a personalized certification logo that includes the MOS logo and the specific programs in which you have achieved certification. If you achieve MOS certification in multiple programs, you can include multiple certifications in one logo.

For more information

To learn more about the Microsoft Office Specialist exams and related courseware, visit:

http://www.certiport.com/mos

Microsoft Office Specialist

Exam 77-728

Excel 2016 Expert: Interpreting Data for Insights

This book covers the skills you need to have for certification as a Microsoft Office Specialist Expert in Excel 2016. Specifically, you need to be able to complete tasks that demonstrate the following skill sets:

1. Manage workbook options and settings
2. Apply custom data formats and layouts
3. Create advanced formulas
4. Create advanced charts and tables

With these skills, you can manage, format, populate, and enhance the types of workbooks most commonly used in a business environment.

Prerequisites

We assume that you have been working with Excel 2016 for at least six months and that you know how to carry out fundamental tasks that are not specifically mentioned in the objectives for this Microsoft Office Specialist exam. This level of proficiency includes familiarity with features and tasks such as the following:

- Creating workbooks
- Adding worksheets to existing workbooks
- Copying and moving worksheets
- Inserting and deleting cells, columns, and rows
- Customizing the Quick Access Toolbar and the ribbon
- Freezing panes and splitting the window
- Setting a print area and adding headers and footers
- Changing fonts and cell styles
- Wrapping text within cells
- Creating and editing tables
- Using relative, mixed, and absolute cell references
- Using functions
- Creating and editing charts, and adding data series
- Inserting text boxes, SmartArt, and other images
- Applying styles and effects to objects
- Positioning objects

Exam Strategy For information about the prerequisite tasks, see *MOS 2016 Study Guide for Microsoft Excel* by Joan Lambert (Microsoft Press, 2017).

Objective group 1

Manage workbook options and settings

The skills tested in this section of the Microsoft Office Specialist Expert exam for Microsoft Excel 2016 relate to managing workbook options and settings. Specifically, the following objectives are associated with this set of skills:

1.1 Manage workbooks

1.2 Manage workbook review

Every Excel workbook exists within a larger ecosystem of objects, including templates, macros, and other workbooks. Mastering workbook management requires knowing not only how to connect workbooks with these other objects, but also how to share a workbook's data with other users.

This chapter guides you in studying methods for creating workbooks from templates and saving workbooks as templates, enabling macros and copying them between workbooks, referencing data in tables and in other workbooks, restricting changes to workbook content and structure, managing workbook versions, and configuring formula calculation options.

To complete the practice tasks in this chapter, you need the practice files contained in the **MOSExcelExpert2016\Objective1** practice file folder. For more information, see "Download the practice files" in this book's introduction.

Objective 1.1: Manage workbooks

Save a workbook as a template

A *template* is an Excel document that contains a preset layout—worksheets, labels, formulas, formatting, and styles, for example—that you can use as the basis for new workbooks. A template ensures that distributed worksheet models all have a consistent look. For example, if you need to consolidate budget numbers from various departments, your task will be much easier if all the worksheets have the same layout. To that end, you can provide to each department a budget template containing the worksheet layout you want everyone to use. A template is also useful if you have a workbook structure that you use frequently. Rather than recreating that structure from scratch each time or making a copy of an existing workbook, you can save a template with the structure you want and then create new workbooks directly from that template.

To save a workbook as a template

1. Set up the workbook with the layout and formatting you want to preserve in the template. You can either use an existing workbook or create a new workbook.

2. Display the **Save As** page of the Backstage view.

3. In the file name box, enter a name for the template.

4. In the file type list below the file name box, click **Excel Template (*.xltx)**. If your workbook contains macros, click **Excel Macro-Enabled Template (*.xltm)** instead.

   Tip If you need your template to be compatible with older versions of Excel, save the file as an Excel 97-2003 Template (*.xlt).

5. In the location list, click **This PC**. Excel automatically selects your user account's Documents\Custom Office Templates folder.

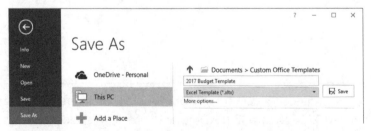

Click This PC to save your template to the Custom Office Templates folder

6. Click **Save**.

To create a new workbook from a custom template

1. Click the **File** tab, and then click **New** to display the New page.

2. On the **New** page, between the search box and the template thumbnails, click **Personal**.

IMPORTANT Depending on the configuration of Excel on your computer, templates will be available under either the Personal or Custom heading. The Featured and Personal or Custom headings appear above the workbook templates only when custom templates are saved on your computer.

Templates that you save in the Custom Office Templates folder are available from the Personal section of the New page of the Backstage view

3. Click the template you want to use. Excel creates a new workbook based on that template.

Hide or display ribbon tabs

The main tabs—such as Home, Insert, and Page Layout—that you see across the top of the ribbon are usually an indispensable part of the Excel interface. However, the display of each of these tabs is optional, which means that if there is a tab you do not use, such as Page Layout or Review, you can temporarily hide it. Also, some third-party apps—for example, QuickBooks—add tabs to the Excel ribbon, and you might prefer not to see these tabs.

After you hide a tab, you can easily display it again if you require any of its commands. Similarly, Excel comes with one tab—the Developer tab—that is hidden by default. If you want to record or write macros, set macro security, or add worksheet controls, you should display this hidden tab for easier access to these and other Excel developer features.

To hide or display ribbon tabs

1. Display the **Customize Ribbon** page of the **Excel Options** dialog box.

In the Main Tabs list, the ribbon's hidden tabs are those with cleared check boxes

2. To display a hidden tab, select its check box; to hide a tab, clear its check box.

3. Click **OK** to close the dialog box and save your changes.

Enable macros in a workbook

Microsoft Visual Basic for Applications (VBA) macros are some of the most useful and most powerful features in the Office 2016 suite. You can use macros to automate repetitive tasks, run a lengthy series of commands with just a few mouse clicks or a keyboard shortcut, create custom Excel functions, and much more. However, this power also means that macros can be used for nefarious purposes, such as trashing files, stealing data, and installing malware. For this reason, when you open a workbook that contains macros, Excel disables those macros by default. You have three choices at this point:

- If the workbook came from a person or source you trust and you were expecting to receive the workbook, you can enable the macros.

- If the workbook came from a person or source you trust but you were *not* expecting to receive the workbook, leave the macros disabled until you can contact the workbook source and ask if they sent it. If they did, you can enable the macros; if they did not, leave the macros disabled.

- If the workbook did not come from a person or source you trust, leave the macros disabled.

When you open a file that uses the Excel Macro-Enabled Workbook (*.xlsm) format or the Excel Macro-Enabled Template (*.xlst) format, Excel displays the Security Warning information bar that tells you the workbook's macros have been disabled.

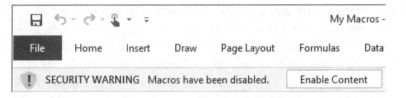

When you open a macro-enabled Excel workbook, click Enable Content only if you trust the document

To enable macros in a workbook

→ To enable macros in a workbook that displays the Security Warning information bar, if you trust the workbook, click **Enable Content** to enable the macros; otherwise, close the information bar to leave the macros disabled.

→ To enable macros in a workbook after you have already closed the Security Warning information bar, click the **File** tab, and on the **Info** page, click the **Enable Content** button, and then click **Enable All Content**.

Enabling macros in a trusted workbook

Copy macros between workbooks

If you receive a workbook that contains one or more macros that you find useful, you can continue to run those macros from within that workbook. However, you might find it useful or necessary to copy those macros to one of your own workbooks. For example, if you have a workbook that you keep open all the time, you might prefer to run the macros from that workbook rather than always having to keep the original workbook open. Similarly, many macros make use of an Excel object named ThisWorkbook, which refers to the workbook in which the macro is running. The only way to get such a macro to run successfully in another workbook is to copy it to that file.

You can make all your macros easily and conveniently available by storing them in a special file called the Personal Macro Workbook. However, before you can use this file, you must create it by recording a macro and using the Personal Macro Workbook to store the resulting code. After you have created the Personal Macro Workbook, it will appear in the Visual Basic Editor's Project Explorer pane, so you can follow the steps from the procedure for copying macros to copy macros to the Personal Macro Workbook.

Tip Although you will be able to see the Personal Macro Workbook in the Visual Basic Editor, the workbook does not appear within the regular Excel interface because it is hidden by default. To unhide it, on the View tab, in the Windows group, click Unhide, click PERSONAL (or PERSONAL.XLSB), and then click OK. To hide it again, switch to the Personal window, click View, and then click Hide.

To copy a macro module from one workbook to another

1. Open the workbook that contains the macros you want to copy.

2. Open or create a macro-enabled workbook to which you want to copy the macros.

   IMPORTANT If you create a new workbook to hold the macros, when you save the file, be sure to use the Save As Type list to select the Excel Macro-Enabled Workbook (*.xlsm) file format.
   ---

3. Do either of the following to open the Visual Basic Editor:

   - On the **Developer** tab, in the **Code** group, click **Visual Basic**.
   - Press **Alt+F11**.

4. In the **Project Explorer** pane, locate the workbook that contains the macros you want to copy, and then open that workbook's branches until you see the contents of the **Modules** folder.

   Tip If the Project Explorer pane isn't open, click View and then click Project Explorer, or press Ctrl+R.
   ---

5. Drag the module you want to copy to the **VBAProject** branch of your other workbook. Excel copies the module, creating the Modules branch in the other workbook if necessary.

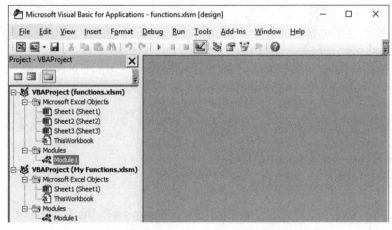

To copy macros, use the Project Explorer pane to drag a module from one workbook to another

To create the Personal Macro Workbook folder

1. In any workbook, on the **Developer** tab, in the **Code** group, click **Record Macro**.

2. In the **Record Macro** dialog box, in the **Store macro in** list, click **Personal Macro Workbook**, and then click **OK**.

To create the Personal Macro Workbook, select it as the storage location for a recorded macro

3. Perform any task, such as selecting a cell or applying a format, and then click **Stop Recording**.

Reference data in another workbook

If you have data in one workbook that you want to use in another, you can set up a link between the two workbooks. This enables your formulas to use references to cells or ranges in the other workbook. When the other data changes, Excel automatically updates the link. You set up links by creating an external reference to a cell or range in the other workbook. The workbook that contains the external reference is called the *dependent workbook* (or the *client workbook*). The workbook that contains the original data is called the *source workbook* (or the *server workbook*).

You can also construct such references manually if you're familiar with the structure of an external reference, by using the following syntax:

   'path[workbookname]sheetname'!reference

The following list describes the arguments:

- **path** The drive and directory in which the workbook is located, which can be a local path, a network path, or even an Internet address. You need to include the path only when the workbook is closed.

- **workbookname** The name of the workbook, including the file extension. Always enclose the workbook name in square brackets ([ ]).

- **sheetname** The name of the worksheet tab that contains the referenced cell.

- **reference** A cell or range reference, or a defined name.

Tip If the *path*, *workbookname*, or *sheetname* contains one or more spaces, or if the workbook is closed, you must enclose all three in a pair of single quotation marks.

The purpose of a link is to avoid duplicating formulas and data in multiple workbooks. If one workbook contains the information you need, you can use a link to reference the data without re-creating it in another workbook. To be useful, however, the data in the dependent workbook should always reflect what actually is in the source workbook. You can make sure of this by updating the link.

To create a link that references data in another workbook

1. Open the source workbook that contains the data you want to reference.

2. In the dependent workbook, start a formula and stop at the point where you want the external reference to appear.

3. On the **View** tab, in the **Window** group, click **Switch Windows**, and then click the source workbook.

4. In the source workbook, click the cell you want to reference in your formula. Excel inserts the external reference into your formula.

Start a formula (cell B3 in the back workbook), switch to the other workbook, and then click the cell you want to reference (cell N3 in the front workbook)

5. Complete your formula, and then press **Enter**.

To update a link

Tip If the source and dependent workbooks are both open, Excel automatically updates the link whenever the data in the source file changes.

➔ Open the dependent workbook. If the source workbook is open when you do so, Excel automatically updates the link.

➔ Open the dependent workbook. If the source workbook is closed when you do so, Excel displays a security warning in the information bar, which tells you that automatic updating of links has been disabled. Click **Enable Content**.

→ On the **Data** tab, in the **Connections** group, click **Edit Links**. In the **Edit Links** dialog box that opens, click the link, and then click **Update Values**.

Source	Type	Update	Status
Division1.xlsx	Worksheet	A	Unknown

Edit Links   ?   ✕

Update Values
Change Source...
Open Source
Break Link
Check Status

Location: C:\Users\Paul\OneDrive\Documents\Workbooks\Budgeting
Item:
Update: ● Automatic   ○ Manual

Startup Prompt...   Close

Use the Edit Links dialog box to update the linked data in the source workbook

Reference table data by using structured references

When you need to reference part of a table in a formula, you could use a cell or range reference that points to the area within the table that you want to use in your calculation. That works, but it suffers from the same problem caused by using cell and range references in regular worksheet formulas: the references often make the formulas difficult to read and understand. The solution for a regular worksheet formula is to replace cell and range references with defined names. For a table, you can use *structured references*. Excel offers a set of defined names—also called *specifiers*—for various table elements (such as the data, the headers, and the entire table), and it automatically creates names for the table fields. You can include these names in your table formulas to make your calculations much easier to read and maintain.

First, here are the predefined specifiers that Excel offers for tables:

- **#All** The entire table, including the column headers and total row
- **#Data** The table data (that is, the entire table, not including the column headers and total row)
- **#Headers** The table's column headers
- **#Totals** The table's total row
- **@** The table row in which the formula appears

Most table references start with the table name (as shown on the Design tab, in the Table Name box). In the simplest case, you can use the table name by itself. For example, the following formula counts the numeric values in a table named *Table1*:

=COUNT(Table1)

If you want to reference a specific part of the table, you must enclose that reference in square brackets after the table name. For example, the following formula calculates the maximum data value in a table named *Sales*:

=MAX(Sales[#Data])

Tip You can also reference tables in other workbooks by using the following syntax: *'Workbook'!Table*. Replace *Workbook* with the workbook file name, and replace *Table* with the table name.

Using the table name by itself is equivalent to using the #Data specifier. So, for example, the following two formulas produce the same result:

=MAX(Sales[#Data])

=MAX(Sales)

Excel also generates column specifiers based on the text in the column headers. Each column specifier references the data in the column, so it does not include the column's header or total. For example, suppose you have a table named *Inventory*, and you want to calculate the sum of the values in the field named *Qty On Hand*. The following formula does this:

=SUM(Inventory[Qty On Hand])

If you want to refer to a single value in a table field, you need to specify the row you want to work with. Here's the general syntax for this:

Table[[Row],[Field]]

Here, replace *Table* with the table name, *Row* with a row specifier, and *Field* with a field specifier. For the row specifier, you have only two choices: the current row and the totals row. The current row is the row in which the formula resides, and you use the @ specifier (or *#ThisRow*) to designate the current row. In this case, however, you use @ followed by the name of the field in square brackets, like this:

@[Standard Cost]

For example, in a table named *Inventory* with a field named *Standard Cost*, the following formula multiplies the Standard Cost value in the current row by 1.25:

*=Inventory[@[Standard Cost]] * 1.25*

IMPORTANT If your formula references a cell in a row other than the current row or the totals row, you must use a regular cell reference (such as *A3* or *D6*).

For a cell in the totals row, use the #Totals specifier, as in this example:

=Inventory[[#Totals],[Qty On Hand]] - Inventory[[#Totals],[Qty On Hold]]

Finally, you can also create ranges by using structured table referencing. As with regular cell references, you create a range by inserting a colon between two specifiers. For example, the following reference includes all the data cells in the Inventory table's Qty On Hold and Qty On Hand fields, and also the data cells in the fields that lie between these two fields, if any:

Inventory[[Qty On Hold]:[Qty On Hand]]

To reference table data by using structured references

1. Start a formula and stop at the point where you want the structured reference to appear.

2. Enter the name of the table that contains the data you want to reference, followed by a left square bracket ([).

3. Enter the source row, field, cell, or predefined specifier.

4. Enter the right square bracket (]).

5. Complete the formula, and then press **Enter**.

Objective 1.1 practice tasks

The practice files for these tasks are located in the **MOSExcelExpert2016\Objective1** practice file folder. The folder also contains result files that you can use to check your work.

➤ Open the **ExcelExpert_1-1a** workbook and do the following:

❑ Save the workbook as a template named <u>MyTemplate</u>.

❑ Use the *MyTemplate* template to create a new Excel workbook.

❑ Save the workbook as <u>MyMacros</u> in the macro-enabled format.

➤ Open the **ExcelExpert_1-1b** workbook and do the following:

❑ Enable macros in the workbook.

❑ Open the Visual Basic Editor and copy the macros from the **ExcelExpert_1-1b** workbook to the *MyMacros* workbook, and then close the Visual Basic Editor.

❑ Return to the *MyMacros* workbook and save it.

❑ Record a simple macro and store it in the Personal Macro Workbook.

❑ Return to the Visual Basic Editor, copy the macros from the *MyMacros* workbook to the Personal Macro Workbook, and then close the Visual Basic Editor.

❑ Unhide the Personal Macro Workbook, then hide it again.

➤ Reopen the **ExcelExpert_1-1a** workbook and do the following:

❑ In cell A2, enter = to start a formula.

❑ Switch to the **ExcelExpert_1-1b** workbook and click cell A1 on Sheet1.

❑ Confirm your external reference formula.

➤ Save the **ExcelExpert_1-1a** workbook. Open the **ExcelExpert_1-1a_results** workbook. Compare the two workbooks to check your work.

➤ Switch to the **ExcelExpert_1-1b** workbook and do the following:

❑ For the table in the Inventory worksheet, in cell G1, create a formula that uses a structured reference to return the sum of the values in the Qty On Hand field.

❑ In cell G2, create a formula that returns the smallest value in the List Price field.

❑ Add a column named Discount and populate it with formulas that multiply the values in the Standard Cost column by 0.75.

➤ Save the **ExcelExpert_1-1b** workbook. Open the **ExcelExpert_1-1b_ results** workbook. Compare the two workbooks to check your work. Then close the open workbooks.

Objective 1.2: Manage workbook review

1

Restrict editing

When you have labored long and hard to get your worksheet formulas or formatting just right, the last thing you need is to have a cell or range accidentally deleted or copied over. You can prevent this problem by using Excel's worksheet protection features, which you can use to prevent changes to anything from a single cell to an entire workbook.

For protecting cells, Excel offers two techniques:

- **Protection formatting** When you use this technique, you format those cells in which you want to allow editing as unlocked, and you format all other cells as locked. You can also hide the formulas in one or more cells if you don't want users to see them. You then turn on worksheet protection, which means that locked cells can't be changed, deleted, moved, or copied over, and that hidden formulas are no longer visible.

- **Protect a range with a password** When you use this technique, you protect one or more ranges with a password, and then specify which users are allowed or denied editing privileges on that range.

By default, all worksheet cells are formatted as locked and their formulas are visible. Note, however, that "locked" in this context really only means that the cells have the potential to be locked. That's because Excel doesn't perform the actual lock—that is, it doesn't prevent users from modifying the cells—until you turn on worksheet protection. With this in mind, here are the options you have when setting up your protection formatting:

- If you want to protect every cell, you can leave the formatting as it is and turn on worksheet protection.

- If you want only certain cells to be unlocked (for data entry, for example), you can select those cells and unlock them before turning on worksheet protection. Similarly, if you want certain formulas hidden, you can select the cells and hide their formulas.

- If you want only certain cells to be locked, first select all the cells and unlock them. Then select the cells you want protected and lock them. To keep only selected formulas visible, hide every formula and then make the formulas you want visible.

If you don't want to protect the entire worksheet, you can restrict your protection to a more targeted area. That is, if you want to prevent unauthorized users from editing within a specific range, you can set up that range with a password. After you protect the sheet, only authorized users who know the password can edit the range.

When you set up protection formatting on one or more cells, or protect one or more ranges with a password, your restrictions don't go into effect until you activate worksheet protection.

To unlock worksheet cells

1. Select the cells you want to unlock.

2. On the **Home** tab, in the **Cells** group, click **Format**, and then click to deactivate the Lock Cell command.

To lock only certain worksheet cells

1. Select all the cells in the worksheet.

2. On the **Home** tab, click **Format**, and then click to deactivate the Lock Cell command.

3. Select the cells you want to lock.

4. On the **Home** tab, click **Format**, and then click to activate the Lock Cell command.

To hide formulas in worksheet cells

1. Select the cells that contain the formulas you want to hide.

2. On the **Home** tab, click **Format**, and then click **Format Cells**.

3. In the **Format Cells** dialog box, on the **Protection** tab, select the **Hidden** check box, and then click **OK**.

To show only certain formulas in worksheet cells

1. Select all the cells in the worksheet.

2. On the **Home** tab, click **Format**, and then click **Format Cells**.

3. In the **Format Cells** dialog box, on the **Protection** tab, select the **Hidden** check box, and then click **OK**.

4. On the worksheet, select the cells that contain the formulas you want to show.

5. On the **Home** tab, click **Format**, and then click **Format Cells**.

6. In the **Format Cells** dialog box, on the **Protection** tab, clear the **Hidden** check box, and then click **OK**.

IMPORTANT Formatting protection doesn't go into effect until you activate worksheet protection.

To protect a range with a password

1. On the **Review** tab, in the **Changes** group, click **Allow Users to Edit Ranges**.

2. In the **Allow Users to Edit Ranges** dialog box, click **New** to open the New Range dialog box.

3. In the **Title** box, enter a name for the range.

4. In the **Refers to cells** box, enter or select the range you want to protect.

5. In the **Range password** box, enter a password.

New Range

Title:

Budget Formulas

Refers to cells:

=A1:F1

Range password:

•••••••••

Permissions...   OK   Cancel

Name, specify, and password-protect a range in the New Range dialog box

6. If you want the password requirement to apply to only specific users or groups, click **Permissions**, and then in the **Permissions** dialog box, do the following:

   a. Click **Add**, enter the name of a user or group, and then click **OK** to add the user or group to the Permissions dialog box.

   b. Click the user or group, and then for the **Edit range without a password** permission, select the **Deny** check box.

   c. Click **OK** to return to the New Range dialog box.

7. In the **New Range** dialog box, click **OK**, reenter the password to confirm it, and then click **OK**. Excel adds the range to the Allow Users To Edit Ranges dialog box.

Your protected ranges appear in the Allow Users To Edit Ranges dialog box

8. Repeat steps 2 through 7 to protect other ranges, and then click **OK** to close the dialog box and save your changes.

IMPORTANT The range password doesn't go into effect until you activate worksheet protection.

To activate worksheet protection

1. Do either of the following to open the Protect Sheet dialog box:

   - On the **Review** tab, in the **Changes** group, click **Protect Sheet**.

   - If the Allow Users To Edit Ranges dialog box is open, click the **Protect Sheet** button in that dialog box.

2. In the **Protect Sheet** dialog box, do the following, and then click **OK**:

   a. Select the **Protect worksheet and contents of locked cells** check box.

   b. If you want, for added security, enter a password in the **Password to unprotect sheet** box. This means that no one can turn off the worksheet's protection without first entering the password.

c. In the **Allow all users of this worksheet to** list, select the check box beside each action you want unauthorized users to be allowed to perform.

Protect Sheet ? ✕

☑ Protect worksheet and <u>c</u>ontents of locked cells

<u>P</u>assword to unprotect sheet:

| |

All<u>o</u>w all users of this worksheet to:

☑ Select locked cells
☑ Select unlocked cells
☐ Format cells
☐ Format columns
☐ Format rows
☐ Insert columns
☐ Insert rows
☐ Insert hyperlinks
☐ Delete columns
☐ Delete rows

OK   Cancel

Activate your protection formatting or range passwords in the Protect Sheet dialog box

3. If you entered a password, reenter the password, and then click **OK** to continue working in the worksheet.

Protect workbook structure

When you protect a workbook's structure, Excel takes the following actions:

- Disables most of the worksheet-related commands on the ribbon. For example, on the Home tab, on the Format menu, the Rename Sheet and Move Or Copy Sheet commands are unavailable.

- Disables most of the commands on the worksheet tab's shortcut menu, including Insert, Delete, Rename, and Move or Copy.

- Keeps the Scenario Manager from creating a summary report.

To protect the workbook structure

1. In the workbook you want to protect, on the **Review** tab, in the **Changes** group, click **Protect Workbook** to display the Protect Structure And Windows dialog box.

Use the Protect Structure And Windows dialog box to prevent changes to your workbook's formatting and worksheet structure

2. Select the **Structure** check box.

3. Enter an optional password in the **Password** text box, and then click **OK**.

4. If you specified a password, reenter the password to confirm, and then click **OK**.

Encrypt a workbook with a password

For a workbook with confidential data, merely protecting cells or sheets might not be enough. For a higher level of security, you can encrypt the workbook with a password. This prevents anyone who doesn't know the password from opening the workbook.

To encrypt a workbook with a password

1. In the workbook you want to protect, display the **Info** page of the Backstage view.

2. Click **Protect Workbook**, and then click **Encrypt with Password**.

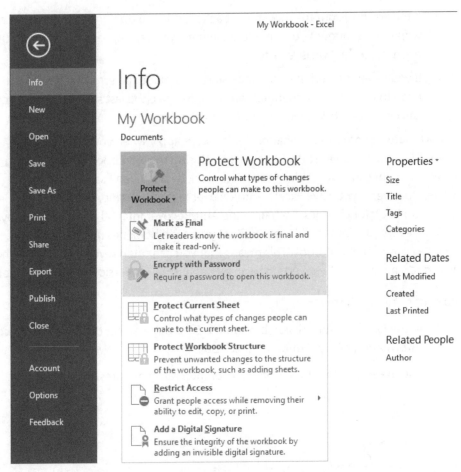

Use the Encrypt With Password command to protect your workbook with a password

3. Enter a password, and then click **OK**.

4. Confirm the password, and then click **OK**.

Manage workbook versions

On occasion, you might realize that you have improperly edited some workbook data, or you have accidentally overwritten an important worksheet range during a paste operation. In some circumstances, you can use the following methods to recover:

- If the improper edit or paste was the most recent action you performed, you can use Undo to reverse the action.

- If the error was not the most recent action, but you don't need to preserve any workbook changes you've made since then, you can repeatedly use Undo until the mistaken action is reversed.

- If you haven't saved the workbook since you made the error, and you don't need to preserve any changes you've made since the last save operation, you can close the workbook without saving it.

Unfortunately, these three scenarios don't always apply when you want to revert a workbook to an earlier state. For example, closing the workbook without saving changes might cause you to lose too much work if you haven't saved the file in a while. However, if you have Excel's AutoRecover feature running, Excel is monitoring your workbook for changes. Each time the AutoRecover interval ends (which is, by default, every 10 minutes), if Excel sees that your workbook has unsaved changes, it saves a copy of the workbook. This means that you can often reverse an error without losing too much work by reverting to an earlier autosaved version of the workbook.

To configure AutoRecover

1. In the **Excel Options** dialog box, on the **Save** page, select the **Save AutoRecover information every X minutes** check box.

2. Use the arrows to set the AutoRecover interval, in minutes.

Use the Save page of the Excel Options dialog box to configure the AutoRecover settings

3. To have Excel preserve the most recent autosaved version of any workbook that you close with unsaved changes, select the **Keep the last autosaved version if I close without saving** check box.

4. In the **AutoRecover file location** box, you can optionally enter the path of a different folder in which Excel should store the autosaved versions.

5. Click **OK**.

To revert to an earlier version of a workbook

1. On the **Info** page of the Backstage view, under **Manage Workbook**, click the autosaved version of the workbook to which you want to revert.

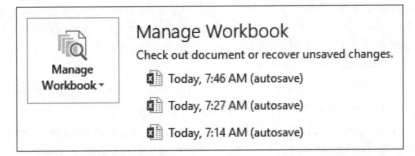

On the Info page, click one of the autosaved versions that appear under the Manage Workbook heading

2. If this is the version you want to recover, display the **Save As** page to save the workbook under a different file name or in a different folder; otherwise, you can return to the most recent version by clicking **Restore** in the information bar.

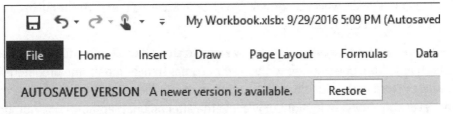

You can return from an autosaved version of a workbook to the most recent version by clicking Restore

Configure formula calculation options

Excel always calculates a formula when you confirm its entry, and the program normally recalculates existing formulas automatically whenever their data changes. This behavior is fine for small worksheets, but it can slow you down if you have a complex model that takes several seconds or even several minutes to recalculate. To turn off this automatic recalculation, Excel gives you two ways to get started:

-   You can use commands on the Calculation Options menu on the Formula tab.
-   You can use settings on the Formulas page of the Excel Options dialog box.

Either way, you're presented with three calculation options:

- **Automatic** This is the default calculation mode; it means that Excel recalculates formulas as soon as you enter them and as soon as the data for a formula changes.

- **Automatic except for data tables** In this calculation mode, Excel recalculates all formulas automatically, except for those associated with data tables. This is a good choice if your worksheet includes one or more massive data tables that are slowing down the recalculation.

- **Manual** Select this mode to force Excel not to recalculate any formulas until you either manually recalculate or save the workbook.

With manual calculation turned on, *Calculate* appears in the status bar whenever your worksheet data changes and your formula results need to be updated.

You can also control various options for iterative calculations. These are calculations where you begin with a guess at the solution, plug that guess into the formula to get a new solution, plug that solution into the formula, and then keep repeating this procedure. Each time you plug a new solution into the formula it is called an *iteration*, so the entire process is called an *iterative calculation*. This type of calculation creates a circular reference, which is normally an error in Excel, so that's why iterative calculations are turned off by default.

How does an iterative calculation know when to stop? If during the iterative process the change from one solution to the next becomes smaller than some predetermined value, the formula is said to have *converged* on the solution. Because the formula might not ever converge—or it might only converge after an unacceptably large number of iterations—you can also tell Excel to stop after a predetermined number of iterations.

To enable the management of iterative calculations, the Formulas tab in the Excel Options dialog box offers two controls:

- **Maximum Iterations** This value is the number of iterations after which Excel must stop the calculation if it hasn't yet converged to a solution. The default value is 100.

- **Maximum Change** This value is the threshold that Excel uses to determine whether the iterative calculation has converged on a solution. If the change in the formula result from one iteration is less than this value, Excel considers the formula solved and stops the iteration. The default value is 0.001, but you can reduce this (for example, to 0.0001 or 0.00001) if you require a solution with more precision.

When performing an iterative calculation, Excel stops the calculation as soon as it hits the Maximum Iterations value or the Maximum Change value (whichever comes first).

To configure the formula calculation options

➜ On the **Formulas** tab, in the **Calculation** group, click **Calculation Options**, and then click **Automatic**, **Automatic Except for Data Tables**, or **Manual**.

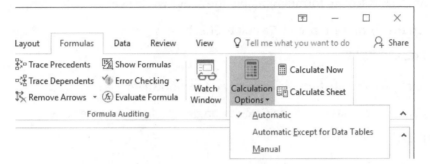

Choose how you want Excel to calculate workbook formulas

Or

1. In the **Excel Options** dialog box, on the **Formulas** page, under **Workbook Calculation,** select the option you want.

2. If you select the **Manual** option and want to run the calculation automatically when you save the file, select the **Recalculate workbook before saving** check box.

Tell Excel how to calculate workbook formulas

3. Click **OK**.

To manually recalculate a single formula

1. Select the cell containing the formula.

2. Click in the formula bar, and then press **Enter** or click the **Enter** button.

To manually recalculate formulas in a selected cell range

1. Display the **Replace** tab of the **Find and Replace** dialog box:

2. Enter an equal sign (=) in both the **Find What** and **Replace With** boxes.

3. Click **Replace All**.

Tip This procedure doesn't actually change any formulas, but it forces Excel to recalculate each formula.

To manually recalculate formulas in only the active worksheet

→ On the **Formulas** tab, click **Calculate Sheet**.

→ Press **Shift+F9**.

To manually recalculate formulas in every open worksheet

→ On the **Formulas** tab, in the **Calculation** group, click **Calculate Now**.

→ Press **F9**.

To manually recalculate every formula in every open worksheet

→ Press **Ctrl+Alt+Shift+F9**.

Tip Excel supports multithreaded calculation on computers with either multiple processors or processors with multiple cores. For each processor (or core), Excel sets up a thread (a separate process of execution). Excel can then use each available thread to process multiple calculations concurrently. For a worksheet with multiple, independent formulas, this can dramatically speed up calculations. To verify that multithreaded calculation is turned on, display the Advanced page of the Excel Options dialog box and, in the Formulas section, ensure that the Enable Multi-Threaded Calculation check box is selected.

To enable and configure iterative calculations

1. In the **Excel Options** dialog box, on the **Formulas** page, select the **Enable iterative calculation** check box.

2. In the **Maximum Iterations** box, enter or select the number of iterations Excel can try before it must stop the calculation.

3. In the **Maximum Change** box, enter the numeric value that you want Excel to use as a threshold to determine whether the calculation has converged on a solution.

Enable and configure iterative calculations on the Formulas page of the Excel Options dialog box

4. Click **OK**.

Objective 1.2 practice tasks

The practice files for these tasks are located in the **MOSExcelExpert2016\ Objective1** practice file folder. The folder also contains result files that you can use to check your work.

➤ Open the **ExcelExpert_1-2a** workbook and do the following:

❑ Unlock the cells in the range C3:C7.

❑ Activate worksheet protection. Do not enter a password. Do not allow users to select locked cells or to format cells.

❑ Ensure that users can modify the loan parameters in the range C3:C7, but cannot change anything else on the worksheet.

❑ Save the **ExcelExpert_1-2a** workbook.

❑ Open the **ExcelExpert_1-2a_results** workbook. Compare the two workbooks to check your work. Then close the open workbooks.

➤ Open the **ExcelExpert_1-2b** workbook and do the following:

❑ Unlock the cells in the range B2:B6.

❑ Protect the cells in the range B7:B8 with the password <u>MOS123</u>.

❑ Protect the worksheet with the same password.

❑ Configure the workbook so that users can change the content of the cells in the range B2:B6.

❑ Configure the workbook so that users cannot change the formulas in the range B7:B8 without first entering the password.

❑ Save the **ExcelExpert_1-2b** workbook.

❑ Open the **ExcelExpert_1-2b_results** workbook. To unlock the range and sheet, use the password <u>mos</u>. Compare the two workbooks to check your work.

❑ Close the **ExcelExpert_1-2b_results** workbook, but leave the **ExcelExpert_1-2b** workbook open for later use.

➤ Open the **ExcelExpert_1-2c** workbook and do the following:

❑ Protect the workbook structure with the password MOS123.

❑ Encrypt the workbook with the same password, and then save and close the workbook.

❑ Reopen the **ExcelExpert_1-2c** workbook and verify that you must enter the password to open the workbook.

❑ Add a worksheet to the workbook. Verify that you must enter the password before you can change the workbook structure in this way.

❑ Save the **ExcelExpert_1-2c** workbook.

❑ Open the **ExcelExpert_1-2c_results** workbook. To open the workbook and unlock the structure, use the password mos. Compare the two workbooks to check your work.

➤ Switch to the **ExcelExpert_1-2b** workbook and do the following:

❑ Change the AutoRecover interval to one minute.

❑ Edit any cell in the range B2:B6.

❑ Don't save your changes to the workbook. Wait for at least one minute to give Excel time to autosave a version of the unsaved workbook.

❑ Display the workbook versions, and then restore the workbook to the version prior to when you made your edit.

➤ In Excel, verify that formula calculations are set to automatic and iterative calculations are turned off.

➤ Open the **ExcelExpert_1-2d** workbook, dismiss the circular reference warning, and do the following:

❑ Change the formula calculation method to Manual, and turn on iterative calculations.

❑ Select cell C6, which contains the circular reference formula, and manually calculate the formula result.

❑ Open the **ExcelExpert_1-2d_results** workbook. Compare the two workbooks to check your work.

❑ To preserve the initial circular reference, close the **ExcelExpert_1-2d** workbook without saving it.

➤ Close the open workbooks.

Objective group 2

Apply custom data formats and layouts

The skills tested in this section of the Microsoft Office Specialist Expert exam for Microsoft Excel 2016 relate to creating custom number formats, performing data validation, applying conditional formatting, and creating custom styles and theme elements. Specifically, the following objectives are associated with this set of skills:

2.1 Apply custom data formats and validation

2.2 Apply advanced conditional formatting and filtering

2.3 Create and modify custom workbook elements

2.4 Prepare a workbook for internationalization

Many worksheets are drab, lifeless conglomerations of numbers, formulas, and text. If you'll be sharing your worksheets with other people, your numbers will have much more impact and will be more easily understood if they're pleasingly formatted and presented in a way that aids comprehension.

This chapter guides you in studying methods for creating number formats; using advanced Fill Series options; configuring data validation; creating and managing conditional formatting rules; creating cell styles, themes, and theme elements; recording and editing simple macros; using form controls; and working with international formats.

> To complete the practice tasks in this chapter, you need the practice files contained in the **MOSExcelExpert2016\Objective2** practice file folder. For more information, see "Download the practice files" in this book's introduction.

Objective 2.1: Apply custom data formats and validation

Create custom data formats

One of the best ways to improve the readability of your worksheets is to display your data in a format that is logical, consistent, and straightforward. Formatting currency amounts with leading dollar signs, percentages with trailing percent signs, and large numbers with commas are a few of the ways you can improve your spreadsheet style. However, you can use Excel to go beyond these built-in formats to create custom number and date formats with which you can display your worksheet values exactly as you want them to be seen.

Excel's built-in numeric formats give you a great deal of control over how your numbers are displayed, but they have their limitations. For example, there is no built-in format you can use to display a different currency symbol, such as the Euro symbol (€), or display temperatures using, say, the degree symbol (°).

To overcome these limitations, you need to create your own custom numeric formats. You can do this either by editing an existing format or by entering your own format from scratch. The formatting syntax and symbols are explained in detail later in this section.

Every Excel numeric format, whether built-in or customized, has the following syntax:

positive format;negative format;zero format;text format

The four parts, separated by semicolons, determine how various numbers are presented. The first part defines how a positive number is displayed, the second part defines how a negative number is displayed, the third part defines how zero is displayed, and the fourth part defines how text is displayed. If you leave out one or more of these parts, numbers are controlled as shown in the following table.

Number of parts used	Format syntax
Three	*positive format;negative format;zero format*
Two	*positive and zero format;negative format*
One	*positive, negative, and zero format*

The following table lists the special symbols you use to define each of these parts.

Symbol	Description
#	Holds a place for a digit and displays the digit exactly as typed. Displays nothing if no number is entered. For example, if a cell's custom format is ### and you enter *25* into the cell, Excel displays *25*.
0	Holds a place for a digit and displays the digit exactly as typed. Displays zero if no number is entered. For example, if a cell's custom format is *000* and you enter *25* into the cell, Excel displays *025*.
?	Holds a place for a digit and displays the digit exactly as typed. Displays a space if no number is entered. For example, if a cell's custom format is *0???* and you enter *25* into the cell, Excel displays *0 25*.
. (period)	Sets the location of the decimal point. For example, if a cell's custom format is *#.#0* and you enter *34.5* into the cell, Excel displays *34.50*.
, (comma)	Sets the location of the thousands separator. Marks only the location of the first thousand. For example, if a cell's custom format is *#,###* and you enter *12345* into the cell, Excel displays *12,345*.
%	Multiplies the number by 100 (for display only) and adds the percent (%) character. For example, if a cell's custom format is *#%* and you enter *.75* into the cell, Excel displays *75%*.
E+ e+ E- e-	Displays the number in scientific format. E- and e- place a minus sign in the exponent; E+ and e+ place a plus sign in the exponent. For example, if a cell's custom format is *0.00E+00* and you enter *123456789* into the cell, Excel displays *1.23E+08*. Similarly, if a cell's custom format is *0.0E-00* and you enter *0.0000012* into the cell, Excel displays *1.2E-06*.
/ (slash)	Sets the location of the fraction separator. For example, if a cell's custom format is *0/0* and you enter *.75* into the cell, Excel displays *3/4*.
$ ( ) : - + <space>	Displays the character. For example, if a cell's custom format *is $##0.00* and you enter *123.5* into the cell, Excel displays *$123.50*.
*	Repeats whatever character immediately follows the asterisk until the cell is full. Doesn't replace other symbols or numbers. For example, you can create a dot trailer in a cell by adding **.* to the format. So if the custom format is *#*.* and you enter *123* into the cell, Excel displays *123............* (where the dots continue until the cell is filled).
_ (underscore)	Inserts a blank space the width of whatever character follows the underscore, which can often help you to align your numbers. For example, the custom format *_(#.00* inserts a blank space the width of the opening parenthesis at the beginning of the displayed value.

2

Symbol	Description
\ (backslash)	Inserts the character that follows the backslash. See the next item for an example. In general, you need to use the backslash only for reserved characters (such as # or @) because if you just enter a single character by itself, Excel will display that character. For example, if a cell's custom format is #.##M and you enter 1.23 into the cell, Excel displays 1.23M.
"text"	Inserts the text that appears within the quotation marks. For example, if a cell's custom format is "Part "\#00-0000 and you enter 123456 into the cell, Excel displays Part #12-3456.
@	Displays the cell's text. For example, if a cell's custom format is @" entry" and you enter credit into the cell, Excel displays credit entry.
[color]	Displays the cell contents in the specified color. For example, if the cell's custom format is 0.00[green];0.00[red], Excel displays positive cell values in green and negative cell values in red. The predefined color values you can use are black, white, red, green, blue, yellow, magenta, and cyan, and the color codes color8 through color55.

Although the built-in date and time formats of Excel are fine for most purposes, you might need to create your own custom formats. For example, you might want to display the day of the week (for example, "Friday"). Custom date and time formats generally are simpler to create than custom numeric formats. There are fewer formatting symbols, and you usually don't need to specify different formats for different conditions. The following table lists the date and time formatting symbols.

Symbol	Description
Date Formats	
d	Day number without a leading zero (1 to 31)
dd	Day number with a leading zero (01 to 31)
ddd	Three-letter day abbreviation (Mon, for example)
dddd	Full day name (Monday, for example)
m	Month number without a leading zero (1 to 12)
mm	Month number with a leading zero (01 to 12)
mmm	Three-letter month abbreviation (Aug, for example)
mmmm	Full month name (August, for example)
yy	Two-digit year (00 to 99)
yyyy	Full year (1900 to 2078)

Symbol	Description
Time Formats	
h	Hour without a leading zero (*0* to *24*)
hh	Hour with a leading zero (*00* to *24*)
m	Minute without a leading zero (*0* to *59*)
mm	Minute with a leading zero (*00* to *59*)
s	Second without a leading zero (*0* to *59*)
ss	Second with a leading zero (*00* to *59*)
AM/PM, am/pm, A/P	Displays the time using a 12-hour clock
/ : . —	Symbols used to separate parts of dates or times
[color]	Displays the date or time in the color specified

The best way to become familiar with custom formats is to try your own experiments. Excel stores each format that you try. If you find that your list of custom formats is getting a bit unwieldy or that it's cluttered with unused formats, you can delete those formats.

To open the Format Cells dialog box

→ On the **Home** tab, in the **Cells** group, click **Format**, and then click **Format Cells**.

→ Right-click the cell or range, and then click **Format Cells**.

→ Press **Ctrl+1**.

To create and apply a custom number format

1. Select the cell or range of cells you want the new format to apply to.

2. Open the **Format Cells** dialog box.

3. On the **Number** tab, in the **Category** list, click **Custom**.

4. To base the custom number format on an existing format, click the base format in the **Type** list.

5. Edit or enter the symbols that define the number format.

2

Define custom number formats in the Type box

6. When you are done, click **OK** to return to the worksheet.

To delete custom number formats

1. Display the **Number** tab of the **Format Cells** dialog box.

2. In the **Category** list, click **Custom**.

3. In the **Type** list, click the format you want to remove.

Tip You can delete only custom formats; you can't delete built-in formats.

---

4. Click **Delete** to remove the format from the list.

5. Click **OK** to close the Format Cells dialog box and return to the worksheet.

Populate cells by using advanced Fill Series options

Worksheets often use text series (such as *January, February, March*; or *Sunday, Monday, Tuesday*) and numeric series (such as *1, 3, 5*; or *2016, 2017, 2018*). Instead of entering these series manually, you can create them automatically by using the Auto Fill feature. That is, you enter and select the first couple of values in the series, drag the fill handle over the range you want to fill, and then click Fill Series in the AutoFill Options list.

	A	B	C	D
1	January			
2	February			
3	March			
4	April			
5	May			
6	June			
7	July			
8				
9		○ Copy Cells		
10		◉ Fill Series		
11		○ Fill Formatting Only		
12		○ Fill Without Formatting		
13		○ Fill Months		
14		○ Flash Fill		
15				
16				

You can use the fill handle and the Fill Series option to extend an existing series

Instead of using the fill handle to create a series, you can use the Series command to gain more control over the process. By using the Series command, you can specify a direction for the fill (rows or columns); a step value (the value by which each item in the series is changed to produce the next item); a stop value (the value at which Excel should terminate the series); whether you want the series to extend the trend of the initial values; the date units (such as day or month) for a date series; and the series type, which can be one of the following four values:

- **Linear** This option finds the next series value by adding the step value to (or subtracting the step value from) the preceding value in the series.
- **Growth** This option finds the next series value by multiplying the preceding value by the step value.
- **Date** This option creates a series of dates based on the option you select in the Date Unit group (Day, Weekday, Month, or Year).
- **AutoFill** This option works much like the fill handle. You can use it to extend a numeric pattern or a text series (for example, Qtr1, Qtr2, Qtr3).

To populate cells by using the Fill Series command

1. Enter the starting value in the first cell you want to use for the series. If you want to create a series out of a particular pattern (such as 2, 4, 6, and so on), fill in enough cells to define the pattern.

2. Select the entire range you want to fill.

37

3. On the **Home** tab, in the **Editing** group, click **Fill**, and then click **Series** to open the Series dialog box.

In the Series dialog box, specify the type of series you want to use to fill the cells

4. Do either of the following to create the series, starting from the active cell:

   - Click **Rows** to create the series in rows.

   - Click **Columns** to create the series in columns.

5. In the **Type** group, click the type of series you want.

6. Do any of the following:

   - If you selected the Date type, click an option in the **Date Unit** group.

   - If you selected the Linear or Growth type and want to extend a series trend, select the **Trend** check box.

   - If you selected a Linear, Growth, or Date series type, enter a number in the **Step value** box. This number is what Excel uses to generate the next value in the series.

   - To place a limit on the series, enter a number in the **Stop value** box.

7. Click **OK** to fill in the series and return to the worksheet.

Configure data validation

Formulas are only as good as the data they're given. For basic data entry errors (for example, entering the wrong date or transposing a number's digits), there's not much you can do other than exhort yourself or the people who use your worksheets to enter data carefully. Fortunately, you have a bit more control when it comes to preventing the entry of improper data such as data that is the wrong type (for example, entering text in a cell that requires a number) or data that falls outside of an allowable range (for example, entering 200 in a cell that requires a number between 1 and 100).

You can prevent these kinds of improper entries, to a certain extent, by adding comments that describe what is allowable inside a particular cell. However, this requires other people to both read and act on the comment text. You can also use custom numeric formatting to "format" a cell with an error message if the wrong type of data is entered. This is useful, but it works only for certain kinds of input errors.

The best solution for preventing data entry errors is to use the data-validation feature of Excel. With data validation, you create rules that specify exactly what kind of data can be entered and in what range that data can fall. You can also specify pop-up input messages that appear when a cell is selected, and error messages that appear when data is entered improperly.

You configure data-validation rules on the Settings tab of the Data Validation dialog box. The following validation types are available:

- **Any Value** Allows any value in the range (that is, it removes any previously applied validation rule). If you're removing an existing rule, be sure to also clear the input message, if any.)

- **Whole Number** Allows only whole numbers (integers). You use the Data list to select a comparison operator (such as Between, Equal To, or Less Than) and then enter the specific criteria. For example, if you click the Between option, you must enter Minimum and Maximum values.

- **Decimal** Allows decimal numbers or whole numbers. You use the Data list to select a comparison operator and then enter the specific numeric criteria.

- **List** Allows only values specified in a list. You specify the allowable values in the Source box on the Settings tab of the Data Validation dialog box, either by specifying a range on the same sheet or a range name on any sheet that contains the list of allowable values (preceding the range or range name with an equal sign) or by entering the allowable values directly into the Source box (separated by commas). You have the option of allowing the user to select from the allowable values by using a drop-down list.

- **Date** Allows only dates. (If the user includes a time value, the entry is invalid.) You use the Data list to select a comparison operator and then enter the specific date criteria (such as a Start date and an End date).

- **Time** Allows only times. (If the user includes a date value, the entry is invalid.) You use the Data list to select a comparison operator and then enter the specific time criteria (such as a Start time and an End time).

- **Text Length** Allows only alphanumeric strings of a specified length. You use the Data list to select a comparison operator and then enter the specific length criteria (such as Minimum and Maximum lengths).

- **Custom** You can use this option to enter a formula that specifies the validation criteria. You can either enter the formula directly into the Formula box on the Settings tab of the Data Validation dialog box (again preceding the formula with an equal sign) or enter a reference to a cell that contains the formula. For example, if you're restricting cell A2 and you want to be sure the entered value is not the same as what's in cell A1, you would enter the formula =A2<>A1.

On the Settings tab of the Data Validation dialog box, set up the criteria for your validation rule

To configure data validation for a cell or range

1. Select the cell or range to which you want to apply the data-validation rule.

2. On the **Data** tab, in the **Data Tools** group, click **Data Validation** to open the Data Validation dialog box.

3. On the **Settings** tab, in the **Allow** list, click one of the validation types.

4. Enter the validation criteria you require.

5. To allow blank entries, either in the cell itself or in other cells specified as part of the validation settings, leave the **Ignore blank** check box selected. If you clear this check box, Excel treats blank entries as zero and applies the validation rule accordingly.

6. If the range had an existing validation rule that also applied to other cells, you can apply the new rule to those other cells by selecting the **Apply these changes to all other cells with the same settings** check box.

7. If you want a message to appear when the user selects the restricted cell or any cell within the restricted range, on the **Input Message** tab, do the following:

   a. Verify that the **Show input message when cell is selected** check box is selected.

   b. In the **Title** box, enter a title for the message.

   c. In the **Input message** box, enter the message that you want Excel to display. For example, you could use the message to give the user information about the type and range of allowable values.

You can configure an input message to appear when a workbook user selects the cell

8. If you want a dialog box to appear when the user enters invalid data, click the **Error Alert** tab, and then do the following:

   a. Select the **Show error alert after invalid data is entered** check box.

   b. In the **Style** list, click the error style you want: Stop, Warning, or Information.

   c. In the **Title** box, enter a title for the message.

   d. In the **Error message** box, enter the message that you want Excel to display.

IMPORTANT Only the Stop style prevents users from entering invalid data.

You can configure an error alert to appear when a workbook user enters an invalid entry

9. Click **OK** to apply the data-validation rule.

Objective 2.1 practice tasks

The practice file for these tasks is located in the **MOSExcelExpert2016 \Objective2** practice file folder. The folder also contains a result file that you can use to check your work.

➤ Open the **ExcelExpert_2-1** workbook, display the **Custom Data Formatting** worksheet, and do the following:

❑ Select cells A1:A4. Create and apply a custom number format that displays the thousands separator, always displays at least one number, displays a leading minus sign and red text if a negative number is entered, displays 0 if 0 is entered, and displays the message Enter a number if a non-numeric value is entered.

❑ Select cell B1. Create and apply a custom number format that displays the thousands separator and the decimal point, always displays at least one digit before and after the decimal point, and displays °C (the degree symbol and the letter C, for *degrees Celsius*) at the end.

❑ Select cells C1:C2. Create and apply a custom number format that displays a six-digit entry with a dash after the first two digits, the text Acct # before the digits, and the text Enter numbers only if the user includes any non-numeric characters in the entry.

❑ Select cell D1. Create and apply a custom date format that displays the two-digit month, day, and year, separated by periods.

❑ Select cell E1. Create and apply a custom time format that displays the two-digit hour and minute with nothing in between them, followed by a space and the text *hours*.

➤ Display the **Fill Series** worksheet and do the following:

❑ In column A, below the *Linear* label, create a linear series that begins at 0, has a step value of 5, and has a stop value of 50.

❑ In column B, below the *Growth* label, create a growth series that begins at 1, has a step value of 2, and has a stop value of 250.

❑ Fill the range C2:C11 with a Date series that uses a day unit and a step value of 2.

❑ Fill the range D2:D11 with a Date series that uses a weekday unit and a step value of <u>1</u>.

❑ Fill the range E2:E11 with a Date series that uses a month unit and a step value of <u>6</u>.

➤ Display the Data Validation worksheet and do the following:

❑ Select cell B2. Create and apply a data-validation rule that restricts data entry to values between 0 and 1 (that is, between 0% and 100%).

❑ Include an input message titled <u>Interest Rate</u> with the following text: *Please enter a value between 0 and 1.*

❑ Then enter a stop-style error message titled <u>Invalid Interest Rate</u> with the following text: *The interest rate value you entered is invalid. Please enter a value between 0 and 1.*

❑ Select cell B3. Create and apply a data-validation rule that restricts data entry to positive values with a minimum of 1 and a maximum of 30.

❑ Include an input message titled <u>Loan Period</u> with the following text: *Please enter a value between 1 and 30 years.*

❑ Then enter a stop-style error message titled <u>Invalid Loan Period</u> with the following text: *The loan period value you entered is invalid. Please enter a value between 1 and 30 years.*

❑ Select cell B4. Create and apply a data-validation rule that restricts data entry to positive values.

❑ Include an input message titled <u>Loan Principal</u> with the following text: *Please enter a value greater than 0.*

❑ Enter a stop-style error message titled <u>Invalid Loan Principal</u> with the following text: *The loan principal value you entered is invalid. Please enter a value greater than 0.*

➤ Save the workbook.

➤ Open the **ExcelExpert_2-1_results** workbook. Compare the two workbooks to check your work. Then close the open workbooks.

Objective 2.2: Apply advanced conditional formatting and filtering

Create custom conditional formatting rules

Many Excel worksheets contain hundreds of data values. You can make sense of large sets of data by creating formulas, applying functions, and performing data analysis. However, there are times when you don't want to analyze a worksheet per se. Instead, all you want are answers to simple questions such as the following:

- Which cell values are less than 0?
- What are the top 10 values?
- Which cell values are above average, and which are below average?

These simple questions aren't easy to answer just by glancing at the worksheet, and the more numbers you're dealing with, the harder it gets. To help you "eyeball" your worksheets and answer these and similar questions, Excel lets you apply *conditional formatting* to the cells. This is a special format that Excel only applies to cells that satisfy some condition, which Excel calls a *rule*. For example, you could apply formatting to show all the negative values in a red font, or you could apply a filter to show only the top 10 values.

There are five types of conditional formatting rules you can apply:

- **Highlight cells rules** A *highlight cell* rule is one that applies a format to cells that meet specified criteria. You have seven choices: Greater Than, Less Than, Between, Equal To, Text That Contains, A Date Occurring, and Duplicate Values. In each case, you use a dialog box to specify the condition and the formatting that you want applied to cells that match the condition.

	A	B	C	D	E	F	G	H	I	J
	Sales Rep	2015	2016	Change						
	Nancy Freehafer	$ 996,336	$ 960,492	-4%						
	Andrew Cencini	$ 606,731	$ 577,983	-5%						
	Jan Kotas	$ 622,781	$ 967,580	55%						
	Mariya Sergienko	$ 765,327	$ 771,399	1%						
	Steven Thorpe	$ 863,589	$ 827,213	-4%						
	Michael Neipper	$ 795,518	$ 669,394	-16%						

Less Than dialog box:
Format cells that are LESS THAN:
`0` with `Light Red Fill with Dark Red Text`
OK   Cancel

For a Less Than conditional formatting rule, the specified formatting is applied to all cells that have a value that is less than the value specified in the dialog box

- **Top/bottom rules** A *top/bottom* rule is a filtering rule that applies a format to cells that rank in the top or bottom (for numerical items, the highest or lowest) values in a range. You can select the top or bottom either as an absolute value (for example, the top 10 items) or as a percentage (for example, the bottom 25%). You can also filter cells that are above or below the average. In each case, you use a dialog box to set up the specifics of the rule. For the Top 10 Items, Top 10%, Bottom 10 Items, and Bottom 10% rules, you use the dialog box to specify the condition and the formatting you want applied to cells that match the condition. For the Above Average and Below Average rules, you use the dialog box to specify the formatting only.

An example of a Top 10 conditional formatting rule

- **Data bars** If you're interested in the *relationship* between similar values in a worksheet, you need some way to visualize the relative values in a range, and that's where data bars are useful. *Data bars* are colored, horizontal bars that appear "behind" the values in a range. (They're like a bar chart.) Their key feature is that the length of the data bar that appears in each cell is related to the value in that cell: the larger the value, the longer the data bar. The cell with the highest value has the longest data bar, and the data bars that appear in the other cells have lengths that reflect their values. Excel configures its default data bars with the longest data bar based on the highest value in the range, and the shortest data bar based on the lowest value in the range. However, you can also set up data bars based on a specific range of values (for example, the values *0* and *100* for test scores) or as a percentage of the largest value.

You can apply data bars by using either a gradient fill or a solid fill

- **Color scales** The color scales in Excel are useful if you want to get a "big picture" view of your data that shows, for example, the overall distribution of the
values and whether there are any *outliers* (values that are much higher or lower
than all or most of the other values). The color scales are also quite helpful if
you want to make value judgments about your data. For example, high sales
and low numbers of product defects are "good," whereas low margins and high
employee turnover rates are "bad." A *color scale* is similar to a data bar in that
it compares the relative values of cells in a range. Instead of bars in each cell,
though, you see cell shading, where the shading color reflects the cell's value.
For example, the lowest values might be shaded red; higher values might be
shaded light red, then orange, yellow, and lime green; and finally the highest
values could be shaded deep green.

*A Green - Yellow - Red color scale shows the lowest values in the deepest shade of red and the highest
values in the deepest shade of green*

- **Icon sets** You use *icon sets* to visualize the relative values of cells in a range.
Excel adds a particular icon to each cell in the range, and that icon tells you
something about the cell's value relative to the rest of the range. For example,
the highest values might get an upward-pointing arrow, the lowest values a
downward-pointing arrow, and the values in between a horizontal arrow. Icon
sets take advantage of symbols that people have strong associations with.

For example, a check mark means something is good or finished or acceptable,
whereas an X means something is bad or unfinished or unacceptable; a green
circle is positive, whereas a red circle is negative (similar to traffic lights).

*A 3 Arrows icon set indicates low, middle, and high values in a data set by using arrows of different
colors and directions*

To create a custom conditional formatting rule

1. Select the range to which you want the custom conditional formatting applied.

2. On the **Conditional Formatting** menu, click **New Rule** to open the New Formatting Rule dialog box.

3. In the **Select a Rule Type** group, click the type of rule you want to apply.

New Formatting Rule	?	✕

Select a Rule Type:

- ▸ Format all cells based on their values
- ▸ Format only cells that contain
- ▸ Format only top or bottom ranked values
- ▸ Format only values that are above or below average
- ▸ Format only unique or duplicate values
- ▸ Use a formula to determine which cells to format

Edit the Rule Description:

Format values that rank in the:

Top ⌄	10	☐ % of the selected range

Preview: No Format Set   Format...

OK   Cancel

The controls in the Edit The Rule Description area vary depending on the rule type you select

4. Select the rule type's conditions and formatting, as required.

5. Click **OK** to close the dialog box and return to the workbook.

Create conditional formatting rules that use formulas

Excel comes with another conditional formatting component that makes this feature even more powerful: you can apply conditional formatting based on the results of a formula. In particular, you can set up a logical formula as the conditional formatting criterion. If that formula returns TRUE, Excel applies the formatting to the cells; if the formula returns FALSE, instead, Excel doesn't apply the formatting.

When comparing worksheet values in a conditional formatting rule's logical formula, you generally set up the expression to compare the value you seek with a specific value from the range, and then use a mixed-reference format for that specific value, so that Excel can compare all the values in the range to the target value. For example, suppose you have a list of percentage increases in the range D5:D13, and a "target" percentage in cell D2. You want to apply a format only on those entries where the percentage increase is greater than or equal to the target value. Here's the logical formula to use:

=$D5 >= $D$2

The mixed-reference format $D5 tells Excel to keep the column (D) fixed while varying the row number (in this example, 5 through 13), and in each case compare the resulting cell value with the value in $D$2.

To create a custom conditional formatting rule based on a formula

1. Select the range to which you want the custom conditional formatting applied.

2. In the **New Formatting Rule** dialog box, in the **Select a Rule Type** list, click **Use a formula to determine which cells to format**.

3. In the **Format values where this formula is true** box, enter your logical formula.

You can create custom conditional formatting rules based on logical formulas

4. Click **Format** to open the Format Cells dialog box.

5. On the **Number**, **Font**, **Border**, and **Fill** tabs, specify the formatting you want Excel to apply when the formula evaluates to TRUE, and then click **OK**.

6. In the **New Formatting Rule** dialog box, click **OK**.

Manage conditional formatting rules

Conditional formatting rules are extremely useful and powerful tools, so you might find that you use them frequently. As you use them, however, your need to manage those rules will increase. For example, you'll often need to edit existing rules to update the conditions or change the formatting. Similarly, if you've applied two or more rules to the same range, you need to know how to change the order that Excel uses to apply those rules. Finally, you also need to know how to delete existing rules that you no longer require.

To edit a conditional formatting rule

1. Click any cell in the range that has the conditional formatting applied.

2. On the **Conditional Formatting** menu, click **Manage Rules** to open the Conditional Formatting Rules Manager dialog box.

3. Click the rule you want to modify, and then click **Edit Rule** to open the Edit Formatting Rule dialog box.

4. Make your changes to the rule type, rule conditions, or rule formatting, and then click **OK**.

5. In the **Edit Formatting Rule** dialog box, click **OK**.

6. In the **Conditional Formatting Rules Manager** dialog box, click **OK**.

To change the order in which conditional formatting rules are applied

1. Click any cell in the range that has the conditional formatting applied.

2. Open the **Conditional Formatting Rules Manager** dialog box.

3. Click a rule, and then click either the up arrow or the down arrow until the rule is in the position you prefer.

4. Repeat for the other rules you want to move, and then click **OK**.

To delete a conditional formatting rule

1. Click any cell in the range that has the conditional formatting applied.

2. Open the **Conditional Formatting Rules Manager** dialog box.

3. Click the rule you want to remove, and then click **Delete Rule**. Excel removes the rule.

4. Click **OK** to close the dialog box and return to the worksheet.

> **Tip** If you want to delete multiple rules, a quicker method is to click any cell in the range that has the rules applied, click the Home tab, click Conditional Formatting in the Styles group, click Clear Rules, and then click Clear Rules From Selected Cells. If you want to delete every rule in the current worksheet, click Clear Rules From Entire Sheet.

Objective 2.2 practice tasks

The practice files for these tasks are located in the **MOSExcelExpert2016 \Objective2** practice file folder. The folder also contains result files that you can use to check your work.

➤ Open the **ExcelExpert_2-2a** workbook and do the following:

❑ On the **Student Grades** worksheet, for the cells in the Grade column, create and apply a custom conditional formatting rule that applies the 4 Traffic Lights Icon Set formatting based on the cell values. Display the black icon for values less than 50; the red icon for values from 50 to 59; the yellow icon for values from 60 to 79; and the green icon for values of 80 and greater.

❑ On the **Projects** worksheet, for the cells in the Percent column, create and apply a custom conditional formatting rule that applies the Data Bar format with a green gradient fill based on the cell values. Set the minimum value to 0 and the maximum value to 1.

❑ On the **Product Inventory** worksheet, for the Product Name column, create and apply a custom conditional formatting rule that applies an Orange fill color to cells that contain duplicate product names.

❑ Save the workbook.

❑ Open the **ExcelExpert_2-2a_results** workbook. Compare the two workbooks to check your work, and then close the open workbooks.

➤ Open the **ExcelExpert_2-2b** workbook and do the following:

❑ On the **Customers** worksheet, for the cell range A4:K94, create and apply a formula-based conditional formatting rule that evaluates cell B1 and applies a Yellow fill color to all the cells of each row that has the same country/region in column I. Test the conditional formatting rule by changing the country/region in cell B1.

❑ On the **Accounts Receivable Data** worksheet, for the cell range A4:G55, use the MOD function (refer to Excel Help if you are not familiar with this function) to create and apply a formula-based conditional formatting rule that applies a Light Gray, Background 2 fill color to every other row. Test the conditional formatting rule by deleting a row.

❑ On the **Products** worksheet, for the cell range A2:B78, create and apply a formula-based conditional formatting rule that applies a Red fill color and Bold font to the cells in the rows that contain the highest and lowest values in the Change In Units Sold column. Test the conditional formatting rule by entering new high and low values.

❑ Save the workbook.

❑ Open the **ExcelExpert_2-2b_results** workbook. Compare the two workbooks to check your work, and then close the open workbooks.

➤ Open the **ExcelExpert_2-2c** workbook, display the **Accounts Receivable Data** worksheet, and do the following for the cell range A4:G55:

❑ Create and apply a conditional formatting rule that applies a Light Green fill color to the cells in each row that has an Invoice Amount value greater than $2,000.

❑ Create and apply a conditional formatting rule that applies an Orange fill color to the cells in each row that has a Days Overdue value greater than or equal to 30.

❑ Edit the first rule so that it applies the formatting to rows that have an Invoice Amount value that is greater than $1,500.

❑ Change the order of the conditional formatting rules so that Excel applies the Invoice Amount rule before it applies the Days Overdue rule.

❑ Save the workbook.

❑ Open the **ExcelExpert_2-2c_results** workbook. Compare the two workbooks to check your work, and then close the open workbooks.

Objective 2.3: Create and modify custom workbook elements

Create and modify cell styles

You can make it easier to format cells the way you want by creating a custom *cell style*, which is a combination of up to six formatting options: the number format; the horizontal and vertical alignment; the font, including the typeface, style, size, color, and text effects; the border; the background color and fill effects; and cell protection.

Excel comes with several dozen predefined cell styles, many of which vary with the document theme. However, Excel also has many cell styles that are independent of the current theme, including styles for sheet titles and headings, and styles that identify totals, calculations, and output cells.

Cell styles can include a number format, alignment, font, borders, fill, and protection formatting

If none of the predefined cell styles is right for your needs, you can use the Format Cells dialog box to apply your own formatting. This dialog box has six tabs—Number, Alignment, Font, Border, Fill, and Protection—which correspond to the six cell style options. You can specify from one to all six style options.

If you want to reuse this formatting in other workbooks, you can save the formatting options as a custom cell style.

Use the Format Cells dialog box to create a custom cell style

To create a custom cell style

1. On the **Home** tab, in the **Styles** group, click **Cell Styles** to open the Cell Styles gallery.

   > **Tip** If you already have a cell that is formatted with some or all of the options you want to use in your custom cell style, select the cell before starting these steps. Excel uses the cell's style options as the defaults for your new custom style.

2. Click **New Cell Style** to open the Style dialog box.

3. Enter a name for the style, and then click **Format** to display the Format Cells dialog box.

4. On the **Number**, **Alignment**, **Font**, **Border**, **Fill**, and **Protection** tabs of the dialog box, select the formatting options you want for your cell style.

5. Click **OK** to return to the Style dialog box.

6. Clear the check box for each of the style options that you don't want to include in your custom style.

7. Click **OK** to save the custom style and display it in the Custom section of the Cell Styles gallery.

To modify a predefined cell style

1. In the **Cell Styles** gallery, right-click the cell style you want to change, and then click **Modify** to open the Style dialog box.

2. Click **Format** to open the Format Cells dialog box.

3. On the **Number**, **Alignment**, **Font**, **Border**, **Fill**, and **Protection** tabs of the dialog box, modify the formatting options for the cell style.

4. Click **OK** to return to the Style dialog box.

5. Clear the check box for each of the style options that you no longer want to include in the style.

6. Click **OK** to close the dialog box and return to the worksheet.

Create custom themes and theme elements

Create and modify custom themes

A *workbook theme* is a predefined collection of color, font, and effect formatting options. Each theme comes with preset formatting in three categories: color scheme, font set, and effects (which includes formatting such as drop shadows and 3D effects). Excel offers more than three dozen predefined themes.

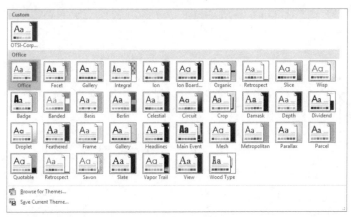

Custom themes appear at the top of the Themes menu, above the 37 built-in themes in the Office gallery

If none of the predefined themes offer the exact formatting you require, you can modify any theme by selecting a different color scheme, font set, or effects scheme. You can even create your own custom color and font sets. However, if you go to all this trouble to get your workbook formatting just right, it is time-consuming to have to repeat the same steps for other workbooks you open or create. To avoid this problem, you can save your theme customizations as a new workbook theme. This enables you to apply the custom formatting to any workbook just by selecting the custom theme.

Exam Strategy The objective domain for Exam 77-728, "Excel Expert 2016: Interpreting Data for Insights," requires you to demonstrate the ability to create custom color schemes, font sets, and themes. You will not be required to customize effect schemes.

Create custom color schemes

Excel offers many tools for turning a plain, unformatted worksheet into an attractive, professional-quality model. For example, features such as custom numeric and date formats and conditional formatting can make your data easier to read and analyze. The final touch involves adding just the right amount of color to your worksheets. With colors, you can emphasize important results, shape the layout of your page, and add subtle psychological effects. Excel comes with nearly two dozen built-in color schemes that make it easy to apply colors to your worksheets.

Custom
▉ ▎▏▍▎▏▉ MOSColors
▉ ▏ ▉▉▉▉ Office-Excel
▉ ▉ ▏▏▏▏ OTSI-Corporate

Office
▉ ▏▎▍▎▏ Office
▉ ▉▉ ▉▉ ▏ Office 2007 - 2010
▉ ▏ ▏▎▉▉ Grayscale
▉ ▉▉ ▉▉ Blue Warm
▉ ▉▉▉ ▏ Blue
▉ ▉▉ ▏▉ Blue II
▉ ▏▉ ▉▉ Blue Green
▉ ▎▏▏▉▉ Green
▉ ▏▏▉▉▉ Green Yellow
▉ ▏▏▎▉▉ Yellow
▉ ▏▉▎▎▉ Yellow Orange
▉ ▏▎▉▉▏ Orange
▉ ▉▉ ▉▉ Orange Red
▉ ▉▉▉ ▉ Red Orange
▉ ▉▎ ▉ Red
▉ ▉▉▉ ▉▉ Red Violet
▉ ▉▉▎▉▉ Violet
▉ ▉▉▉▉ ▏ Violet II
▉ ▏▏▏▏▉ Median
▉ ▏▏▏▏▏ Paper
▉ ▉▉▏▏▉ Marquee
▉ ▉ ▉▎▏ Slipstream
▉ ▉ ▉▉▉ Aspect
C̲ustomize Colors...

Custom color schemes appear at the top of the Theme Colors menu, above the 23 built-in color schemes in the Office gallery

However, if no scheme offers the exact colors you want, you can create your own. Each scheme consists of 12 color elements:

- **Text/Background - Dark 1** The dark text color that Excel applies when you choose a light background color

- **Text/Background - Light 1** The light text color that Excel applies when you choose a dark background color

- **Text/Background - Dark 2** The dark background color that Excel applies when you choose a light text color

- **Text/Background - Light 2** The light background color that Excel applies when you choose a dark text color

- **Accent 1 through Accent 6** The colors that Excel uses for accents, such as chart data markers

- **Hyperlink and Followed Hyperlink** The colors that Excel uses for worksheet links: the former for links that haven't been clicked and the latter for links that have been clicked

To create a custom color scheme, you can replace any of the dozen theme colors with an existing theme color, a standard color, or a custom color

For each element, you can choose a color from the standard color palette, or you can create a custom color. Excel offers two color models:

- **RGB** This color model is based on the idea that you can create any color by combining three base colors: red, green, and blue. You assign a value between 0 and 255 for each color: the higher the number, the more intense the color.

> **Tip** In the RGB color model, when the red, green, and blue values are equal, you get a gray-scale color. Lower numbers produce darker grays, and higher numbers produce lighter grays. Black has RGB values of 0, 0, 0 and white has RGB values of 255, 255, 255.

- **HSL** This color model is based on three properties, each of which is assigned a value between 0 and 255:
  - *Hue* (which is more or less equivalent to the term *color*) measures the position on the color spectrum. Lower numbers indicate a position near the red end, and higher numbers move through the yellow, green, blue, and violet parts of the spectrum.
  - *Saturation* is a measure of the purity of a particular hue, with 255 giving a pure color, and lower numbers indicating that more gray is mixed with the hue until, at 0, the color becomes part of the gray scale.
  - *Luminance* is a measure of the brightness of a color, where lower numbers are darker, and higher numbers are brighter.

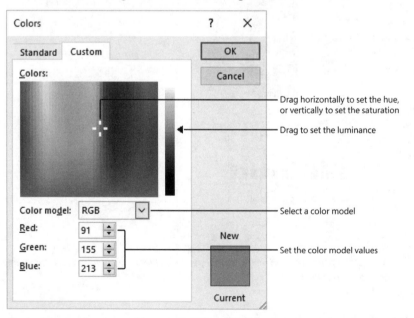

On the Custom tab, you can either specify RGB or HSL values, or you can drag the color pointer and the luminance slider

Create custom font sets

Each Excel theme comes with more than two dozen built-in font sets that make it easy to apply fonts to your worksheets. Each font set defines two fonts: a *+Heading font* that Excel uses for title and heading text; and a *+Body font* that Excel uses for regular worksheet text. The typeface is often the same for both types of text, but some font sets use two different typefaces, such as Cambria for titles and headings and Calibri for body text. If no existing font set includes the typefaces you want, you can create your own.

A custom font set can include any installed fonts

To create a custom color scheme

1. On the **Page Layout** tab, in the **Themes** group, click **Colors**, and then click **Customize Colors** to open the Create New Theme Colors dialog box.

   > **Tip** If an existing color scheme is close to what you want, you can save some time and effort by using that color scheme as your starting point. On the Page Layout tab, in the Themes groups, click Colors, and then click the color scheme to apply it to the workbook and use it as the starting point.

2. For any theme color you want to modify, click the color picker to display a menu of color options, and then do one of the following:

   - In the **Theme Colors** gallery, click one of the 12 existing theme colors or 60 variations to assign it to the color role.
   - In the **Standard Colors** gallery, click one of the 10 standard colors.
   - Click **More Colors** to open the Colors dialog box. On the **Custom** tab, in the **Color model** list, select either **RGB** or **HSL**, do any of the following, and then click **OK**:
     - If you chose RGB, enter specific values for **Red**, **Green**, and **Blue**.
     - If you chose HSL, enter specific values for **Hue**, **Sat**, and **Lum**.
     - To adjust the hue visually, drag the color pointer horizontally.

- ○ To adjust the saturation visually, drag the color pointer vertically.
- ○ To adjust the luminance visually, drag the luminance slider.
3. Repeat step 2 for each theme color you want to modify.
4. In the **Name** box, enter a name for your new color scheme.
5. Click **Save** to save the color scheme and apply it to the worksheet.

To create a custom font set

1. On the **Page Layout** tab, in the **Themes** group, click **Fonts**, and then click **Customize Fonts** to open the Create New Theme Fonts dialog box.
2. In the **Heading font** list, select a font for worksheet headings.
3. In the **Body font** list, select a font for worksheet text.
4. In the **Name** box, enter a name for your new font set.
5. Click **Save** to save the font set and close the dialog box.

To create a custom workbook theme

1. Create a custom color scheme.
2. Create a custom font set.
3. On the **Page Layout** tab, in the **Themes** group, click **Themes**, and then click **Save Current Theme** to open the Save Current Theme dialog box.

IMPORTANT By default, Excel displays the Document Themes folder, which is located in your user profile's AppData\Roaming\Microsoft\Templates folder. Save your theme in this folder to ensure that it gets displayed in the Themes list.

When saving your custom theme, be sure to store it in the Document Themes folder

4. In the **File name** box, enter a name for the custom theme.

5. Click **Save**.

6. To modify the theme, repeat steps 1 through 3.

Create and modify simple macros

One of the secrets of Excel productivity is the automation of routine tasks through the use of command macros. A *command macro* is code that performs an action that has an effect on the Excel environment. For example, the macro might insert text into a worksheet cell or change an Excel option. In general, you can think of a command macro as being akin to a ribbon command. The key is that a single macro can consist of two, three, or even a dozen or more actions, each of which is performed, in sequence, when you run the macro. Macros save time and increase efficiency in two ways:

- **For short tasks that you run frequently** Placing those tasks inside a macro is efficient because you can launch the macro with just one or two clicks or by pressing a keyboard shortcut.

- **For long tasks** Having these tasks in a macro is fast because although the entire procedure might take you several minutes manually, the macro might take only a few seconds.

Although you can create macros manually by using the Microsoft Visual Basic for Applications (VBA) Editor, it is often easier to create a macro by using the Macro Recorder. With this method, you start the recorder, and then you run through the tasks you want to automate (which might include selecting cells, running ribbon commands, and choosing dialog box options). The Recorder translates everything into the appropriate Visual Basic for Applications statements and copies those statements to a macro in a module. You can then use the recorded macro to replay the entire procedure any time you want. After you have recorded a macro, you can modify it by adding a description, assigning a shortcut key, or deleting the macro.

To open the Record Macro dialog box

→ On the **Developer** tab, in the **Code** group, click **Record Macro**.

See Also For information about how to display the Developer tab, see "Hide or display ribbon tabs" in "Objective 1.1: Manage workbooks."

→   Near the left end of the Excel status bar, click the **Macro Recording** button. (If the button isn't on the status bar, right-click the status bar, and then click **Macro Recording.**)

The Macro Recording button

You must provide a name and storage location for the macro before you record it

To record a simple macro

1. Open the **Record Macro** dialog box.

2. In the **Macro name** box, change the name to something memorable or descriptive. You must follow these guidelines when naming your macros:

    -   The name must be 255 or fewer characters.

    -   The first character must be a letter or an underscore (_).

    -   No spaces or periods are allowed.

3. In the **Shortcut key** box, assign an optional shortcut key to the macro.

    IMPORTANT Excel shortcut keys are case-sensitive, which means that you can create separate shortcuts with uppercase and lowercase letters. Also, make sure you don't specify a shortcut key that conflicts with built-in shortcuts (such as Ctrl+B for Bold or Ctrl+C for Copy). If you use a key that clashes with an Excel shortcut, Excel overrides its own shortcut and runs your macro instead (if the workbook containing the macro is open).

4. In the **Store macro in** list, specify where the macro will reside. You can store the macro in the current workbook, a new workbook, or in the Personal Macro Workbook. If you use the Personal Macro Workbook, your macros will be available to all of your workbooks.

5. In the **Description** box, enter an optional description of the macro.

6. Click **OK** to return to the workbook and start recording.

7. Perform the tasks you want to include in the macro. Here are some things to bear in mind during the recording:

   - Excel gives you just one indication that a recording is in progress: the status bar's Macro Recording button changes to a square.

   - Excel makes the mouse available for all actions.

   - Because the Macro Recorder takes note of everything you do, be careful not to perform any extraneous keyboard actions or mouse clicks during the recording.

The Macro Recording button during a recording

During a recording, the Macro Recording status bar button changes to a square

8. When you finish the tasks, do either of the following to stop recording the macro:

   - On the **Developer** tab, in the **Code** group, click **Stop Recording**.

   - On the status bar, click the **Macro Recording** button.

To modify a macro

1. On the **Developer** tab, in the **Code** group, click **Macros** to open the Macro dialog box.

2. Click the macro you want to modify, and then click **Options** to open the Macro Options dialog box.

3. Do any of the following, and then click **Close** to return to the Macro dialog box:

   - In the **Shortcut key: Ctrl+** box, assign a shortcut key to the macro.

   - In the **Description** box, enter a description of the macro.

4. Click **Cancel** to close the Macro dialog box.

To run a macro

➜ In the **Macro** dialog box, click the macro you want to run, and then click **Run**.

➜ If you assigned a shortcut key to the macro, press the shortcut key.

To delete a macro

1. In the **Macro** dialog box, click the macro you want to remove, and then click **Delete**. Excel asks you to confirm.

2. Click **Yes** to delete the macro.

Insert and configure form controls

A useful technique for ensuring accurate data entry is to add an extra worksheet layer that gives the user an interface for entering the data. This interface uses form controls such as lists, check boxes, and option buttons. These controls are linked to specific worksheet cells, and you associate certain values with these controls, which then ensure that the user can enter only the values you want. There are nine control types available.

The worksheet form controls are available in the Form Control gallery

The following table defines the available control types.

Icon	Name	Description
▭	Command button	When the user clicks this button, Excel launches a macro that you have assigned to it. When you add a command button to a worksheet, the Assign Macro dialog box opens, and from there you can either record a new macro or assign an existing macro.
▦	Combo box	This control displays a list from which the user can select an item. The control shows only one item at a time until it is expanded. Items in the list are defined by the values in a specified worksheet range, and the value returned to the linked cell is the number of the item chosen.

Icon	Name	Description
☑	Check box	This control offers an option that the user can switch on or off. On the worksheet, a selected check box stores the value TRUE in its linked cell; if the check box is cleared, it stores the value FALSE.
⬍	Spin button	This type of button displays an upward-pointing arrow and a downward-pointing arrow that, when clicked, increment or decrement (respectively) the value in a linked cell.
▤	List Box	This type of control displays a list from which the user can select an item. The items in the list are defined by the values in a specified worksheet range, and the value returned to the linked cell is the number of the item chosen.
◉	Option Button	When grouped with other option buttons, a button of this type enables the user to select only one of the options. Option buttons work in tandem with group boxes (discussed next), in which the user can select only one of the option buttons within a group box.
⌐XYZ⌐	Group Box	This type of control is a grouping of two or more option buttons. The user can select only one option from the group.
Aa	Label	A label control displays text that names or describes a worksheet form control.
▲▼	Scroll Bar	A scroll bar control resembles a window scroll bar. The user can use this type of scroll bar to select a number from a range of values. Dragging the scroll box changes the value of the control, and this value is what is returned to the linked cell. You can create either a horizontal or a vertical scroll bar.

To insert and configure a form control

1. On the **Developer** tab, in the **Controls** group, click **Insert** to display the Form Controls gallery.

2. Click the control you want to insert. The pointer changes to a crosshair.

3. Drag the pointer on the worksheet to create the control.

4. If you are creating a command button, in the **Assign Macro** dialog box, choose the macro you want to run when the user clicks the button.

Tip To select a control (for example, to move it or resize it), hold down the Ctrl key and then click the control.

---

5. To edit the control caption (if any), right-click the control, click **Edit Text**, adjust the text accordingly, and then click outside the control.

6. Right-click the control, and then click **Format Control** to open the Format Control dialog box.

7. If the dialog box has a **Control** tab, click that tab, and in the **Cell Link** box, enter a reference for the control's linked cell. Some controls (such as the group box and label) don't link to a cell, so you won't see this option.

Tip When working with option buttons, you have to enter only the linked cell for one of the buttons in a group. Excel automatically adds the reference to the rest.

---

8. Configure other options for the control:

- **Checked**   For check boxes and option buttons—click this option to display the control as selected.

- **Unchecked**   For check boxes and option buttons—click this option to display the control as cleared.

- **Input Range**   For list boxes and combo boxes—enter a reference to the worksheet range that contains the items you want to display in the list.

- **Current Value**   For scroll bars and spin buttons—enter the initial value of the scroll bar or spin button.

- **Minimum Value**   For scroll bars and spin buttons—for a scroll bar, enter the value when the scroll box is at its leftmost position (for a horizontal scroll bar) or its topmost position (for a vertical scroll bar); for a spin button, enter its smallest possible value.

- **Maximum Value**   For scroll bars and spin buttons—for a scroll bar, enter the value when the scroll box is at its rightmost position (for a horizontal scroll bar) or its bottommost position (for a vertical scroll bar); for a spin button, enter its largest possible value.

- **Incremental Change**   For scroll bars and spin buttons—for a scroll bar, enter the amount that the value changes when the user clicks on a scroll arrow; for a spin button, enter the amount the value changes when the user clicks an arrow.

- **Page Change**   For scroll bars—enter the amount that the scroll bar's value changes when the user clicks between the scroll box and a scroll arrow.

9. Click **OK**.

Objective 2.3 practice tasks

The practice file for these tasks is located in the **MOSExcelExpert2016 \Objective2** practice file folder. The folder also contains a result file that you can use to check your work.

➤ Open the **ExcelExpert_2-3** workbook, display the **Inventory** worksheet, and do the following:

❑ Create a new cell style named <u>MOSCell</u> that uses a bold, 16-point, Dark Blue font, a Center alignment, and a bottom border. Apply it to the range A1:G1.

❑ Create a custom color scheme named <u>MOSColors</u> and apply it to the workbook.

❑ Create a custom font set named <u>MOSFonts</u> and apply it to the workbook.

❑ Save the custom theme as <u>MOSTheme</u>.

❑ Verify that your custom theme now appears in the Themes gallery.

➤ Display the **Inventory (2)** worksheet and do the following:

❑ Select cell E2 and start recording a macro. Use the default macro name and location settings.

❑ Perform the following actions: apply bold, apply the Currency number format, and center the text within the cell.

❑ Stop the recording.

❑ Select cell F2 and run the macro you just recorded.

➤ Display the **Amortization Schedule** worksheet and do the following:

❑ In cell D3, insert a spin button control. Link the spin button to the Amortization value in cell C3, and configure it with a minimum value of <u>1</u>, a maximum value of <u>30</u>, and an incremental change value of <u>1</u>.

❑ In cell F2, insert a combo box control. Link the combo box to cell G7, and configure it to display the items in cells G3:G6.

➤ Save the **ExcelExpert_2-3** workbook.

➤ Open the **ExcelExpert_2-3_results** workbook. Compare the two workbooks to check your work, and then close the open workbooks.

Objective 2.4: Prepare a workbook for internationalization

If you'll be creating workbooks that will be used internationally, it's a good idea to tailor certain aspects of your worksheet models for your readership. For example, many countries/regions use a period (.) as the thousands separator and a comma (,) as the decimal point. For monetary amounts, you'll need to use the currency symbol that's appropriate to the region, such as the pound (£) or the euro (€) and, in some cases, you'll also need to change the symbol position. In Europe, for example, the euro sign (€) is usually placed after the amount (for example, 50 €), but in some countries/regions—such as the Netherlands—the symbol appears before the amount (for example, € 50). Similarly, date formats are different around the world. In the United States, for example, 12/11/2016 means December 11, 2016; in much of Europe, however, 12/11/2016 is interpreted as the 12th of November, 2016.

To make your documents easier for international readers to interpret, Windows supports different regional settings for various countries. These settings apply to all Windows applications—including Excel—and they set the defaults for such things as number formats and date and time formats.

Choose a region to use its default date and time formats, or select individual formats from the lists

If you change the Windows regional setting, Excel automatically formats your work-sheet date and time values and numeric values by using the appropriate regional settings. However, Excel does *not* automatically apply the regional currency format, so you must format the monetary format manually.

To change the Windows regional data format

1. Display Control Panel.

2. Do either of the following to open the Region dialog box:

    *   In the Category view of Control Panel, click **Clock, Language, and Region**, and then click **Change date, time, or number formats**.

    *   In the Large Icons or Small Icons view of Control Panel, click **Region**.

3. In the **Format** list, select the region you want to use.

4. Click **OK** to close the Region dialog box.

5. Restart Excel to ensure that it uses the new regional setting.

To display a specific date or time in a different international format

1. Select the cell or range you want to format, and open the **Format Cells** dialog box:

2. On the **Number** tab of the dialog box, in the **Category** list, select either **Date** or **Time**.

3. In the **Locale (location)** list, select the international format you want to apply.

4. Click **OK** to close the dialog box.

Tip To ensure that a date or time displays correctly no matter which regional setting Excel is currently using, select one of the formats that appears in the Type list preceded by an asterisk (*).

To apply an international currency format

1. Select the cell or range you want to format.

2. On the **Home** tab in the **Number** group, click **Number Format**, and then click either **Currency** or **Accounting**.

Objective 2.4 practice tasks

The practice file for these tasks is located in the **MOSExcelExpert2016
\Objective2** practice file folder.

➤ Open the **ExcelExpert_2-4** workbook and do the following:

❑ Select the range A2:A11 and apply the *Short Date* number format.

❑ Select the range B2:B11 and apply the *Number* number format.

❑ Select the range C2:C11 and apply the *Currency* number format.

❑ Save the workbook, and then close Excel.

➤ From Control Panel, change the Windows regional data format to one
that uses different date, number, and currency formats than yours.

➤ Reopen the **ExcelExpert_2-4** workbook and do the following:

❑ Verify that the dates in the range A2:A11 now appear in the new
international format.

❑ Verify that the numbers in the range B2:B11 now appear in the new
international format.

❑ Select the range C2:C11. Notice that the currency format did not
automatically update. Reapply the *Currency* number format, and
verify that the monetary values in the range C2:C11 now appear in
the new international format.

❑ Close the workbook.

➤ From Control Panel, change the Windows regional data format to the
one you want to use.

Tip There is no result file for this set of practice tasks because the changes are saved
on your computer rather than in a workbook.

Objective group 3

Create advanced formulas

The skills tested in this section of the Microsoft Office Specialist Expert exam for Microsoft Excel 2016 relate to the advanced use of formulas and data analysis. Specifically, the following objectives are associated with this set of skills:

3.1 Apply functions in formulas

3.2 Look up data by using functions

3.3 Apply advanced date and time functions

3.4 Perform data analysis and business intelligence

3.5 Troubleshoot formulas

3.6 Define named ranges and objects

Although Excel works well as a simple database, in most of your worksheets you'll want to do more than just store data. That is, you'll also want to summarize your data, apply statistical methods, perform data analysis, consolidate multiple worksheets, and perform other techniques that you can use to interrogate your worksheet data and draw conclusions that are relevant to your business requirements. This level of dynamism requires creating worksheet models that use formulas and functions.

This chapter guides you in studying methods for performing logical operations by using functions, nesting functions, performing statistical operations with functions, looking up data with functions, applying advanced date and time functions, analyzing and consolidating data, creating financial formulas, troubleshooting formula errors, and defining named cells, ranges, and tables.

To complete the practice tasks in this chapter, you need the practice files contained in the **MOSExcelExpert2016\Objective3** practice file folder. For more information, see "Download the practice files" in this book's introduction.

Objective 3.1: Apply functions in formulas

Insert functions into a formula

Formulas that combine operators with basic operands such as numeric and string values are the mainstay of any Excel spreadsheet. But to really get the most benefit from the spreadsheet model, you need to expand your formula repertoire to include worksheet functions. Excel includes dozens of these functions, and they're essential to making your worksheet easier to work with and more powerful.

To insert a function into a formula

1. Enter your formula up to the point where you want to insert the function.

2. On the **Formulas** tab, in the **Function Library** group, click the category that contains the function you want to use. Then on the category menu, click the function.

3. In the **Function Arguments** dialog box, enter the function arguments, and then click **OK**.

Perform logical operations by using the IF, AND, OR, and NOT functions

In the computer world, we *very* loosely define something as *intelligent* if it can per-form tests on its environment and act in accordance with the results of those tests. However, a computer is a binary machine, so "acting in accordance with the results of a test" means that it can do only one of two things. However, even with this limited range of options, you can still bring a great deal of intelligence to your worksheets. Your formulas will actually be able to test the values in cells and ranges and then return results based on those tests. This is all done with the logical functions in Excel, which are designed to create decision-making formulas.

The following table describes the most common logical functions.

Function	Description
IF(*logical_test*, *value_if_true*[, *value_if_false*])	Performs a logical test and returns a value based on the result
AND(*logical1*[, *logical2*,...])	Returns TRUE if all the arguments are true
OR(*logical1*[, *logical2*,...])	Returns TRUE if any argument is true
NOT(*logical*)	Reverses the logical value of the argument

You use the IF function to test some condition and then return a value based on the result of that text. This is the simplest version of the IF function:

IF(logical_test, value_if_true)

The *logical_test* argument is a logical expression—that is, an expression that returns TRUE or FALSE (or their equivalent numeric values: 0 for FALSE and any other number for TRUE); the *value_if_true* argument is the value returned by the function if *logical_test* evaluates to TRUE.

For example, suppose cell B2 contains a sales rep's total sales and you want to give the rep a 10-percent bonus if those sales are greater than $100,000. Here's a formula that does that:

*=IF(B2 > 100000, B2 * 0.1)*

The logical expression B1 > 100000 is used as the test. Assume that you add this formula to cell C2. If the logical expression proves to be true (that is, if the value in cell B2 is greater than 100,000), the function returns the value B2 * 0.1—that is, 10 percent of the number in B2—and that's the value you see in cell C2.

C2	▼	⋮	✕	✓	*fx*	=IF(B2 > 100000, B2 * 0.1)	

◢	A	B	C	D	E
1	**Sales Rep**	**Total Sales**	**Bonus**		
2	Victoria Ashworth	$146,621	$14,662		
3	Helen Bennett	$89,226	FALSE		
4	Marie Bertrand	$99,547	FALSE		
5	Aria Cruz	$111,861	$11,186		

A formula that uses the IF function to return a bonus for reps with sales greater than 100,000

When the IF function test returns FALSE (that is, the value in column B is less than or equal to 100,000), the function returns FALSE as its result. That's not inherently bad, but the worksheet would look tidier (and, hence, be more useful) if the formula returned, for instance, the value 0 instead.

To do this, you need to use the full IF function syntax:

IF(logical_test, value_if_true, value_if_false)

The extra *value_if_false* argument is the value returned by the function if *logical_test* evaluates to FALSE. Here's a modification of the sales rep bonus calculation that takes a FALSE result into account:

=IF(B2 > 100000, B2 * 0.1, 0)

It's often necessary to perform an action if and only if two conditions are true. For example, you might want to pay a salesperson a bonus if and only if dollar sales exceed a certain amount *and* unit sales also exceed some minimum value. If the dollar sales, the unit sales, or both fall below the minimum, no bonus is paid. In Boolean logic, this is called an *And* condition because one expression *and* another must be true for a positive result.

In Excel, And conditions are handled by the AND logical function:

AND(logical1[, logical2,...])

Here, *logical1* and *logical2* arguments are the logical conditions to test. (The ellipsis means that you can enter as many conditions as you need.) The AND result is calculated as follows:

- If *all* the arguments return TRUE (or any nonzero number), AND returns TRUE.

- If one or more of the arguments return FALSE (or 0), AND returns FALSE.

Consider a formula that uses AND to check whether a sales rep's sales total is greater than $100,000 and units total is greater than 10,000. That formula could look like this:

=AND(B2 > 100000, C2 > 10000)

D2	▼	⋮	✕	✓	*fx*	=AND(B2 > 100000, C2 > 10000)	
◢	A		B		C	D	E
1	**Sales Rep**		**Total Sales**		**Total Units**	**Bonus**	
2	Victoria Ashworth		$146,621		14,076	TRUE	
3	Helen Bennett		$89,226		5,996	FALSE	
4	Marie Bertrand		$99,547		10,136	FALSE	
5	Aria Cruz		$111,861		10,896	TRUE	

A formula that uses the AND function to test whether the values in columns B and C exceed a specified minimum

In many worksheet models, you need to take an action if one thing *or* another is true. For example, you might want to pay a salesperson a bonus if she exceeds the dollar sales budget *or* if she exceeds the unit sales budget. In Boolean logic, this is called an *Or* condition.

In Excel, Or conditions are handled by the OR function:

OR(logical1[, logical2,...])

Here, *logical1* and *logical2* arguments are the logical conditions to test. (The ellipsis means that you can enter as many conditions as you need.) The OR result is calculated as follows:

- If one or more of the arguments return TRUE (or any nonzero number), OR returns TRUE.

- If *all* of the arguments return FALSE (or 0), OR returns FALSE.

Consider the following formula, which uses OR to check whether a sales rep's sales total is greater than $100,000 or units total is greater than 10,000:

=OR(B2 > 100000, C2 > 10000)

D2	▼	⋮	×	✓	*fx*	=OR(B2 > 100000, C2 > 10000)

◢	A	B	C	D	E
1	**Sales Rep**	**Total Sales**	**Total Units**	**Bonus**	
2	Victoria Ashworth	$146,621	14,076	TRUE	
3	Helen Bennett	$89,226	5,996	FALSE	
4	Marie Bertrand	$99,547	10,136	TRUE	
5	Aria Cruz	$111,861	10,896	TRUE	

A formula that uses the OR function to test whether the values in columns B or C exceed a specified minimum

You sometimes need to return the opposite of a logical expression. For example, you might want to set up a worksheet that looks for the sales reps who did not make their sales quota and then flag those reps for further training. If you have a worksheet that already returns a TRUE or FALSE value based on whether a sales rep meets his quota, flagging whether the sales rep needs more training is a matter of returning the opposite value: if a sales rep meets her quota (TRUE), she doesn't need training (FALSE); if a sales rep doesn't meet his quota (FALSE), he does need training (TRUE).

In Excel, you return the opposite of a logical expression by using the NOT function:

NOT(logical)

Here, the *logical* argument is the logical condition to test. The NOT result is calculated as follows:

- If *logical* is TRUE (or any nonzero number), NOT returns FALSE.

- If *logical* is FALSE (or 0), NOT returns TRUE.

The following formula uses NOT in the Training Required? column (E) to return the opposite of the logical value in the Bonus column (D):

=*NOT(D2)*

E2	▼	⋮	×	✓	*fx*	=NOT(D2)	

◢	A	B	C	D	E
1	**Sales Rep**	**Total Sales**	**Total Units**	**Bonus**	**Training Required?**
2	Victoria Ashworth	$146,621	14,076	TRUE	FALSE
3	Helen Bennett	$89,226	5,996	FALSE	TRUE
4	Marie Bertrand	$99,547	10,136	TRUE	FALSE
5	Aria Cruz	$111,861	10,896	TRUE	FALSE

A formula that uses the NOT function to return the opposite of the logical values in column D

To insert a logical function into a formula

→ On the **Formulas** tab, in the **Function Library** group, click **Logical**, click one of the functions in the list (such as IF, AND, OR, or NOT), and then enter the arguments, if any, as described earlier in this topic.

Perform logical operations by using nested functions

You can create sophisticated logical tests by combining one or more logical functions within a single expression. In particular, you can create complex expressions by including one logical function within another. This is called *nesting*, and the inner function is called a *nested function*.

For example, suppose you want to pay a salesperson a bonus only if both of the following criteria are met:

- The rep exceeds the dollar sales budget *or* the unit sales budget.
- The rep's accounts have a product return rate of less than 10 percent.

Because both criteria must be met, this is a logical And condition, which requires the AND function. However, the first of the criteria is a logical Or condition, so you need to nest an OR function inside the AND function. The following formula does this:

=*AND(OR(B2 > 100000, C2 > 10000), D2 < 0.1)*

E2	▼	:	✕	✓	*fx*	=AND(OR(B2 > 100000, C2 > 10000), D2 < 0.1)

◢	A	B	C	D	E	F
1	**Sales Rep**	**Total Sales**	**Total Units**	**Return Rate**	**Bonus**	
2	Victoria Ashworth	$146,621	14,076	17%	FALSE	
3	Helen Bennett	$89,226	5,996	9%	FALSE	
4	Marie Bertrand	$99,547	10,136	8%	TRUE	
5	Aria Cruz	$111,861	10,896	7%	TRUE	

A formula that uses an OR function nested in an AND function to determine whether a sales rep earns a bonus

To nest logical functions

1. Insert the first logical function into your formula.

2. Enter the function arguments as described earlier in this topic, including the logical function you want to nest as one of the arguments.

Perform statistical operations by using the SUMIFS, AVERAGEIFS, and COUNTIFS functions

You use the SUM, AVERAGE, and COUNT functions in Excel to return the total value, the mean value, and the number of values, respectively, within a specified range. These functions operate over the entire range, but it's often the case that you want the sum, the average, or the count of only those cells that meet some criterion. For example, you might want the total sales for just the customers from the United States. Even more sophisticated calculations are possible when you use multiple criteria. For example, you might want the total sales for those customers who are from the United States and who are based in Oregon.

These seem like they would require complex combinations of the IF, AND, and OR functions nested within with SUM, AVERAGE, or COUNT function. Fortunately, Excel includes three summary functions that you can use to specify multiple criteria without complex nesting: SUMIFS, AVERAGEIFS, and COUNTIFS. In each case, the "IFS" part of the function name implies that one or more IF functions are built in to each function, without being explicitly invoked, as you'll see in the sections that follow.

3

The SUMIFS function sums cells in one or more ranges that meet one or more criteria:

SUMIFS(sum_range, range1, criteria1[, range2, criteria2, ...])

The *sum_range* argument is the range from which the sum values are taken. Excel sums only those cells in *sum_range* that correspond to the cells that meet the criteria. The *range1* argument is the first range of cells to use for the sum criteria, and the *criteria1* argument is the first criterion, entered as text, that determines which cells to sum. Excel applies the criterion to *range1*. You can enter up to 127 range/criterion pairs.

Consider the following SUMIFS function example. In this model, SUMIFS is used to calculate the total bonuses (range E3:E14) just for those sales reps whose total units (range C3:C14) are greater than 10,000:

=SUMIFS(E3:E14, C3:C14, " > 10000")

	A	B	C	D	E
E1		f_x	=SUMIFS(E3:E14, C3:C14, ">10000")		
1	Bonus total for reps with more than 10,000 units:				$32,126
2	Sales Rep	Total Sales	Total Units	Return Rate	Bonus
3	Victoria Ashworth	$146,621	14,076	17%	$0
4	Helen Bennett	$89,226	5,996	9%	$0
5	Marie Bertrand	$99,547	10,136	8%	$9,955
6	Aria Cruz	$111,861	10,896	7%	$11,186
7	Ann Devon	$97,758	8,603	7%	$0
8	Karin Josephs	$80,032	5,314	13%	$0
9	Maria Larsson	$83,565	7,220	8%	$0
10	Elizabeth Lincoln	$101,062	6,419	7%	$10,106
11	Patricia McKenna	$81,241	7,149	10%	$0
12	Liz Nixon	$123,725	9,502	12%	$0
13	Dominique Perrier	$109,848	10,458	7%	$10,985
14	Rene Phillips	$113,612	7,271	12%	$0

A formula that uses SUMIFS to apply a criterion to a sum calculation

The AVERAGEIFS function averages cells in one or more ranges that meet one or more criteria:

AVERAGEIFS(average_range, range1, criteria1[, range2, criteria2, ...])

The *average_range* argument is the range from which the average values are taken.

Excel averages only those cells in *average_range* that correspond to the cells that meet the criteria. The *range1* argument is the first range of cells to use for the average criteria, and the *criteria1* argument is the first criterion, entered as text, that determines which cells to average. Excel applies the criterion to *range1*. You can enter up to 127 range/criterion pairs.

In the following example, AVERAGEIFS is used to calculate the average sales (range B3:B14) just for those sales reps whose total units (C3:C14) are greater than 10,000 and whose return rate (D3:D14) is less than 10 percent:

=AVERAGEIFS(B3:B14, C3:C14, " > 10000", D3:D14, " < 0.1")

	E1		:	X	✓	*fx*	=AVERAGEIFS(B3:B14, C3:C14, ">10000", D3:D14, "<0.1")		
	A		B	C	D	E	F	G
1					Average sales	$107,085		
2	Sales Rep		Total Sales	Total Units	Return Rate	Bonus		
3	Victoria Ashworth		$146,621	14,076	17%	$0		
4	Helen Bennett		$89,226	5,996	9%	$0		
5	Marie Bertrand		$99,547	10,136	8%	$9,955		
6	Aria Cruz		$111,861	10,896	7%	$11,186		
7	Ann Devon		$97,758	8,603	7%	$0		
8	Karin Josephs		$80,032	5,314	13%	$0		
9	Maria Larsson		$83,565	7,220	8%	$0		
10	Elizabeth Lincoln		$101,062	6,419	7%	$10,106		
11	Patricia McKenna		$81,241	7,149	10%	$0		
12	Liz Nixon		$123,725	9,502	12%	$0		
13	Dominique Perrier		$109,848	10,458	7%	$10,985		
14	Rene Phillips		$113,612	7,271	12%	$0		

A formula that uses AVERAGEIFS to apply multiple criteria to an average calculation

The COUNTIFS function counts the number of cells in one or more ranges that meet one or more criteria:

COUNTIFS(range1, criteria1[, range2, criteria2, ...])

The *range1* argument is the first range of cells to use for the count, and the *criteria1* argument is the first criterion, entered as text, that determines which cells to count. Excel applies the criterion to *range1*. You can enter up to 127 range/criterion pairs.

In the following example, COUNTIFS is used to count the number of sales reps whose dollar sales (range B3:B14) are greater than $100,000, whose unit sales (C3:C14) are greater than 10,000, and whose return rate (D3:D14) is less than 10 percent:

=COUNTIFS(B3:B14, " > 100000", C3:C14, " > 10000", D3:D14, " < 0.1")

E1	▼ :	× ✓	fx	=COUNTIFS(B3:B14, ">100000", C3:C14, ">10000", D3:D14, "<0.1")			
⬛	A	B	C	D	E	F	G	H
1				Number of All-Star reps:	2			
2	Sales Rep	Total Sales	Total Units	Return Rate	Bonus			
3	Victoria Ashworth	$146,621	14,076	17%	$0			
4	Helen Bennett	$89,226	5,996	9%	$0			
5	Marie Bertrand	$99,547	10,136	8%	$9,955			
6	Aria Cruz	$111,861	10,896	7%	$11,186			
7	Ann Devon	$97,758	8,603	7%	$0			
8	Karin Josephs	$80,032	5,314	13%	$0			
9	Maria Larsson	$83,565	7,220	8%	$0			
10	Elizabeth Lincoln	$101,062	6,419	7%	$10,106			
11	Patricia McKenna	$81,241	7,149	10%	$0			
12	Liz Nixon	$123,725	9,502	12%	$0			
13	Dominique Perrier	$109,848	10,458	7%	$10,985			
14	Rene Phillips	$113,612	7,271	12%	$0			

A formula that uses COUNTIFS to apply multiple criteria to a count calculation

To insert a SUMIFS function into a formula

→ On the **Formulas** tab, in the **Function Library** group, click **Math & Trig**, click **SUMIFS**, and then enter the arguments, as described earlier in this topic.

To insert an AVERAGEIFS or COUNTIFS function into a formula

→ On the **Formulas** tab, in the **Function Library** group, click **More Functions**, click **Statistical**, click **AVERAGEIFS**, and then enter the arguments, as described earlier in this topic.

Objective 3.1 practice tasks

The practice file for these tasks is located in the **MOSExcelExpert2016 \Objective3** practice file folder. The folder also contains a result file that you can use to check your work.

➤ Open the **ExcelExpert_3-1** workbook and do the following:

❑ On the **Gross Margin** worksheet, add formulas to the Gross Margin field (H7:H14) that calculate the gross margin by subtracting Cost from Retail and then dividing by Cost. To avoid #DIV/0! (division by 0) errors, wrap the calculation inside an IF function that returns the gross margin if Cost is not 0, or the message <u>Cost is 0!</u> otherwise.

❑ On the **Inventory** worksheet, create a formula in cell G1 that uses the SUMIFS function to sum the Qty On Hand range for products with a Product Name value that includes *Soup* and a Qty On Hold value of zero.

❑ On the **Parts** worksheet, create a formula in cell F16 that uses the AVERAGEIFS function to calculate the average of the Gross Margin values for the parts that cost less than $10. Use structured table references in your formula (the table name is *Parts*).

❑ On the **Customers** worksheet, create a formula in cell L1 that uses the COUNTIFS function to return the number of customers with the Country value *United States* and the Region value *OR* (the abbreviation for *Oregon*, not the OR function).

➤ Save the workbook.

➤ Open the **ExcelExpert_3-1_results** workbook. Compare the two workbooks to check your work, and then close the open workbooks.

Objective 3.2: Look up data by using functions

The table—more properly referred to as a *lookup table*—is the key to performing lookup operations in Excel. The most straightforward lookup table structure is one that consists of two columns (or two rows):

- **Lookup column** This column contains the values that you look up. For example, if you were constructing a lookup table for a dictionary, this column would contain the words.

- **Data column** This column contains the data associated with each lookup value. In the dictionary example, this column would contain the definitions.

In most lookup operations, you supply a value that the function locates in the designated lookup column. It then retrieves the corresponding value in the data column.

The lookup table theme has many variations. The lookup table can be one of these:

- **A single column or row** In this case, the lookup operation consists of finding the *n*th value in the column.

- **A range with multiple data columns** For instance, in the dictionary example, you might have a second column for each word's part of speech (noun or verb, for example), and perhaps a third column for its pronunciation. In this case, the lookup operation must also specify which of the data columns contains the value required.

- **An array** In this case, the table doesn't exist on a worksheet but is either an array of literal values or the result of a function that returns an array. The lookup operation finds a particular position within the array and returns the data value at that position.

The VLOOKUP function works by looking in the first column of a table for the value you specify. (The *V* in VLOOKUP stands for *vertical*.) It then looks across to the column that you specify and returns whatever value it finds there.

Here's the full syntax for VLOOKUP:

VLOOKUP(lookup_value, table_array, col_index_num[, range_lookup])

The following table describes the VLOOKUP function arguments.

Argument	Description
lookup_value	The value you want to find in the first column of *table_array*. You can enter a number, string, or reference.
table_array	The cell range or named table to use for the lookup.
col_index_num	The column number in *table_array* that contains the data you want the formula to return (the first column—that is, the lookup column—is 1, the second column is 2, and so on).
range_lookup	A Boolean value that determines how Excel searches for *lookup_value* in the first column. If FALSE, VLOOKUP returns the first exact match for *lookup_value*. If TRUE (the default), if no exact match is found, the function returns the next largest value.

Here are some notes to keep in mind when you work with VLOOKUP:

- If *range_lookup* is TRUE or omitted, you must sort the values in the first column in ascending order.

- If the first column of the table is text, you can use the standard wildcard characters in the *lookup_value* argument (use ? to substitute for individual characters; use * to substitute for multiple characters).

- If *lookup_value* is less than any value in the lookup column, VLOOKUP returns the #N/A error value.

- If VLOOKUP doesn't find a match in the lookup column, it returns #N/A.

- If *col_index_num* is less than 1, VLOOKUP returns #VALUE!; if *col_index_num* is greater than the number of columns in *table_array*, VLOOKUP returns #REF!.

As an example, assume that a worksheet uses a VLOOKUP formula in cell B4 to take the account number entered into cell B2, locate the exact match in the first column of the range D3:E15, and return the account name from the second column in that range. The formula would look like this:

=VLOOKUP(B2, D3:E15, 2, FALSE)

| B4 | ▼ | : | ✕ | ✓ | fx | =VLOOKUP(B2, D3:E15, 2, FALSE) |

⊿	A	B	C	D	E
1					
2	Enter Account Number:	10-0009		**Account Number**	**Account Name**
3				10-0009	Around the Horn
4	Account Name is:	Around the Horn		02-0200	Consolidated Holdings
5				01-0045	Eastern Connection
6				08-2255	Great Lakes Food Market
7				12-1212	Island Trading
8				12-3456	Laughing Bacchus Wine Cellars
9				09-2111	Old World Delicatessen
10				14-1882	Queen Cozinha
11				14-5741	QUICK-Stop
12				07-0025	Rattlesnake Canyon Grocery
13				07-4441	Seven Seas Imports
14				16-6658	Simon's Bistro
15				14-1882	Split Rail Beer & Ale

A formula that uses VLOOKUP to look up an account name for a specified account number

The HLOOKUP function is similar to VLOOKUP except that it searches for the lookup value in the first row of a table. (The *H* in HLOOKUP stands for *horizontal*.) If successful, this function then looks down to the specified row and returns the value it finds there. Here's the syntax for HLOOKUP:

HLOOKUP(*lookup_value, table_array, row_index_num[, range_lookup]*)

The following table describes the HLOOKUP function arguments.

Argument	Description
lookup_value	The value you want to find in the first row of *table_array*. You can enter a number, string, or reference.
table_array	The cell range or named table to use for the lookup.
row_index_num	The row number in the table that contains the data you want the formula to return (the first row—that is, the lookup row—is 1, the second row is 2, and so on).
range_lookup	A Boolean value that determines how Excel searches for *lookup_value* in the first row. If FALSE, HLOOKUP returns the first exact match for *lookup_value*. If TRUE (the default), if no exact match is found, the function returns the next largest value.

As an example, assume that a worksheet uses an HLOOKUP formula in cell C10 to take the month entered into cell C9, locate the exact match in the first row of the range C1:N7, and return the value from the TOTAL row (the seventh row in that range).

The formula would look like this:

=HLOOKUP(C9, C1:N7, 7, FALSE)

| C10 | ▼ | : | ✕ | ✓ | fx | =HLOOKUP(C9, C1:N7, 7, FALSE) | | | | |

⊿	A	B	C	D	E	F	G	H	I	J	K
1		**EXPENSES**	**January**	**February**	**March**	**April**	**May**	**June**	**July**	**August**	**September**
2		**Advertising**	$4,600	$4,200	$5,200	$4,600	$4,200	$5,200	$4,600	$4,200	$5,200
3		**Rent**	$2,100	$2,100	$2,100	$2,100	$2,100	$2,100	$2,100	$2,100	$2,100
4		**Supplies**	$1,300	$1,200	$1,400	$1,300	$1,200	$1,400	$1,300	$1,200	$1,400
5		**Salaries**	$16,000	$16,000	$16,500	$16,000	$16,000	$16,500	$16,000	$16,000	$16,500
6		**Utilities**	$500	$600	$600	$500	$600	$600	$500	$600	$600
7		**TOTAL**	$24,500	$24,100	$25,800	$24,500	$24,100	$25,800	$24,500	$24,100	$25,800
8											
9		**Month**	May								
10		**Total**	$24,100								

A formula that uses HLOOKUP to look up a monthly expenses total for a specified month

The basic lookup procedure—finding a value in a column or row and then returning an offset value—will satisfy most of your needs. However, a few operations require a more sophisticated approach that makes use of two more lookup functions: MATCH and INDEX.

The MATCH function looks through a row or column of cells for a value. If MATCH finds that value, it returns the relative position of the match in the row or column. Here's the syntax:

MATCH(lookup_value, lookup_array[, match_type])

The following table describes the MATCH function arguments.

Argument	Description
lookup_value	The value you want to find. You can use a number, string, reference, or logical value.
lookup_array	The row or column of cells you want to use for the lookup.
match_type	How you want Excel to match the *lookup_value* with the entries in the *lookup_array*. You have three choices: • 0 finds the first value that exactly matches *lookup_value*. The *lookup_array* can be in any order. • 1 finds the largest value that is less than or equal to *lookup_value* (this is the default value). The *lookup_array* must be in ascending order. • -1 finds the smallest value that is greater than or equal to *lookup_value*. The *lookup_array* must be in descending order.

3

Tip You can use wildcard characters within the *lookup_value* argument (provided that *match_type* is 0 and *lookup_value* is text). You can use the question mark (?) for single characters and the asterisk (*) for multiple characters.

Normally, you don't use the MATCH function by itself; you combine it with the INDEX function. INDEX returns the value of a cell at the intersection of a row and column inside a reference. Here's the syntax for INDEX:

INDEX(reference, row_num[, column_num][, area_num])

The following table describes the INDEX function arguments.

Argument	Description
reference	A reference to one or more cell ranges.
row_num	The number of the row in *reference* from which to return a value.
column_num	The number of the column in *reference* from which to return a value. You can omit *column_num* if *reference* is a single column.
area_num	If you entered more than one range for *reference*, *area_num* is the range you want to use. The first range you entered is 1 (this is the default), the second is 2, and so on.

The idea is that you use MATCH to get *row_num* and/or *column_num* (depending on how your table is laid out) and then use INDEX to return the value you need.

For example, consider a worksheet that uses a MATCH and INDEX formula in cell B2 to take the account number entered into cell B1, locate the match in the range H6:H13, and return the quantity from the range C6:C13.

The formula would look like this:

=INDEX(C6:C13, MATCH(B1, H6:H13, 0))

| B2 | ▾ | : | × | ✓ | fx | =INDEX(C6:C13, MATCH(B1, H6:H13, 0)) | | |

◢	A	B	C	D	E	F	G	H
1	**Part Number**	D-178						
2	**Quantity**	57						
3								
4	**Parts Database**							
5	**Division**	**Description**	**Quantity**	**Cost**	**Total Cost**	**Retail**	**Gross Margin**	**Number**
6	4	Gangley Pliers	57	$10.47	$ 596.79	$17.95	71.4%	D-178
7	3	HCAB Washer	856	$ 0.12	$ 102.72	$ 0.25	108.3%	A-201
8	3	Finley Sprocket	357	$ 1.57	$ 560.49	$ 2.95	87.9%	C-098
9	2	6" Sonotube	86	$15.24	$ 1,310.64	$19.95	30.9%	B-111
10	4	Langstrom 7" Wrench	75	$18.69	$ 1,401.75	$27.95	49.5%	D-017
11	3	Thompson Socket	298	$ 3.11	$ 926.78	$ 5.95	91.3%	C-321
12	1	S-Joint	155	$ 6.85	$ 1,061.75	$ 9.95	45.3%	A-182
13	2	LAMF Valve	482	$ 4.01	$ 1,932.82	$ 6.95	73.3%	B-047

A formula that uses MATCH and INDEX to look up a quantity for a specified part number

To insert a VLOOKUP or an HLOOKUP function into a formula

➔ On the **Formulas** tab, in the **Function Library** group, click **Lookup & Reference**, click **VLOOKUP** or **HLOOKUP**, and then enter the arguments, as described earlier in this topic.

To insert the MATCH and INDEX functions into a formula

1. On the **Formulas** tab, in the **Function Library** group, click **Lookup & Reference**, and then click **INDEX**.

2. In the **Select Arguments** dialog box, click **reference,row_num,column_num,area_num**, and then click **OK**.

3. In the **Function Arguments** dialog box, enter the INDEX function arguments, including a MATCH function for the *row_num* and/or *column_num* arguments, and then click **OK**.

3

Objective 3.2 practice tasks

The practice file for these tasks is located in the **MOSExcelExpert2016 \Objective3** practice file folder. The folder also contains a result file that you can use to check your work.

➤ Open the **ExcelExpert_3-2** workbook and do the following:

  ❑ On the **Tax Rate** worksheet, add a formula to cell B18 that uses the tax table in the range C9:F15 to look up the income entered into cell B17 and return the applicable tax rate.

  ❑ On the **Discount Schedule** worksheet, create formulas in the range D3:D10 that use the discount schedule in the range B13:G14 to look up the units ordered from the range A3:A10 and return the applicable discount percentage.

  ❑ On the **Parts** worksheet, add a formula to cell B3 that uses the range A7:H14 to look up the part number entered into cell B1, and then return the corresponding value from the field entered in cell B2.

➤ Save the workbook.

➤ Open the **ExcelExpert_3-2_results** workbook. Compare the two workbooks to check your work, and then close the open workbooks.

Objective 3.3: Apply advanced date and time functions

You can use the date and time functions in Excel to convert dates and times to serial numbers and perform operations on those numbers. This capability is useful for such things as accounts receivable aging, project scheduling, time-management applications, and much more.

Excel uses serial numbers to represent specific dates and times. To get a date serial number, Excel uses December 31, 1899, as an arbitrary starting point and then counts the number of days that have passed since then. For example, the date serial number for January 1, 1900, is 1; for January 2, 1900, it's 2; for June 6, 1944 its 16229, and so on.

To get a time serial number, Excel expresses time as a decimal fraction of the 24-hour day to return a number between 0 and 1. The starting point, midnight, is given the value 0, so noon—halfway through the day—has a serial number of 0.5, and 5:00 PM has a serial number of 0.70833. You can combine the two types of serial numbers. For example, 42735.5 represents noon on December 31, 2016.

The advantage of using serial numbers in this way is that it makes calculations involving dates and times very easy. A date or time is really just a number, so any mathematical operation you can perform on a number can also be performed on a date. This is invaluable for worksheets that track delivery times, monitor accounts receivable or accounts payable aging, and calculate invoice discount dates, for example.

Reference the date and time by using the NOW and TODAY functions

If you need a date for an expression operand or a function argument, you can enter it by hand if you have a specific date in mind. Much of the time, however, you need more flexibility, such as always entering the current date or time.

When you need to use the current date in a formula, a function, or an expression, use the TODAY function, which doesn't take any arguments. This function returns the serial number of the current date, with midnight as the assumed time. For example, on August 22, 2016, the TODAY function returns the serial number 42604.0.

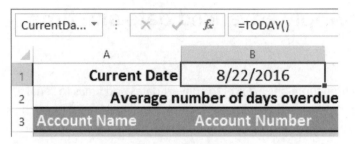

The TODAY function returns the current date serial number in the date format of the cell

Note that TODAY is a dynamic function that doesn't always return the same value. Each time you edit the formula, enter another formula, recalculate the worksheet, or reopen the workbook, TODAY updates its value to return the current system date.

When you need to use the current time in a formula, a function, or an expression, use the NOW function, which doesn't take any arguments. This function returns the serial number of the current time, with the current date as the assumed date. For example, at noon on August 22, 2016, the NOW function returns the serial number 42604.5.

CurrentDa... ▼	⋮	✕	✓	*fx*	=NOW()	
◢		A			B	
1	**Current Date & Time**			8/22/2016 12:02		

The NOW function returns the current date and time serial number in the date/time format of the cell

If you want only the time component of the serial number, subtract TODAY from NOW:

   =NOW - TODAY

Just like the TODAY function, NOW is a dynamic function that doesn't keep its initial value (that is, the time at which you entered the function). Each time you edit the formula, enter another formula, recalculate the worksheet, or reopen the workbook, NOW uptimes its value to return the current system time.

To insert the TODAY or NOW function in a formula

➔ On the **Formulas** tab, in the **Function Library** group, click **Date & Time**, and then click **TODAY** or **NOW**.

Serialize numbers by using date and time functions

The date functions in Excel work with or return date serial numbers. However, you can also work in the opposite direction by taking numbers that represent a specified year, month, and day, and serialize those into a valid Excel date. When you have a date serial number, you can use more Excel date functions to manipulate and perform calculations with those dates.

Similarly, the time functions work with or return time serial numbers, but you can also work in the opposite direction by taking numbers that represent a specified hour, minute, and second, and serialize those into a valid Excel time. When you have a time serial number, you can use other Excel time functions to manipulate and perform calculations with those times.

A date consists of three components: the year, month, and day. It often happens that a worksheet generates one or more of these components, and you need some way of building a proper date out of them. You can do that by using the DATE function:

DATE(year, month, day)

The following table describes the DATE function arguments.

Argument	Description
year	The year component of the date (a number from 1900 through 9999)
month	The month component of the date (a number from 1 through 12)
day	The day component of the date (a number from 1 through 31)

IMPORTANT Different versions of Excel and even different functions within the current version of Excel interpret two-digit years differently. For example, a year entered as 30 might be interpreted as either 1930 or 2030. To avoid problems, always use a four-digit value when entering the year component of any date.

For example, the expression DATE(2016, 12, 25) returns Christmas Day in 2016.

Note, too, that DATE adjusts for wrong month and day values. For example, the expression DATE(2016, 12, 32) returns January 1, 2017. Here, DATE adds the extra day (there are 31 days in December) to return the date of the next day.

The three components of a date—year, month, and day—can also be extracted individually from a specified date. This might not seem all that interesting at first, but actually many useful techniques arise out of working with a date's component parts.

You can extract a date's components by using the YEAR, MONTH, and DAY functions:

YEAR(serial_number)
MONTH(serial_number)
DAY(serial_number)

In each function, *serial_number* is the date (or a string representation of the date) you want to work with. (Remember that, despite its name, *serial_number* is not a date serial number; instead, it's an actual date, such as 8/23/2017.) For example, on August 23, 2017, the expression YEAR(TODAY) returns 2017.

The MONTH function returns a number between 1 and 12 that corresponds to the month component of a specified date. The DAY function returns a number between 1 and 31 that corresponds to the day component of a specified date.

B3	▾	⋮	✕	✓	*fx*	=MONTH($B$1)	

◢	A	B	C	D
1	Date:	August 23, 2017		
2	Year:	2017		
3	Month:	8		
4	Day:	23		

The YEAR, MONTH, and DAY functions return the individual components of a specified date

The WEEKDAY function returns a number that corresponds to the day of the week upon which a specified date falls:

WEEKDAY(serial_number[, return_type])

The following table describes the WEEKDAY function arguments.

Argument	Description
serial_number	The date (or a string representation of the date) you want to work with.
return_type	An integer that determines how the value returned by WEEKDAY corresponds to the days of the week: • A *return_type* of 1 sets the return values to 1 (Sunday) through 7 (Saturday); this is the default. • A *return_type* of 2 sets the return values to 1 (Monday) through 7 (Sunday). • A *return_type* of 3 sets the return values to 0 (Monday) through 6 (Sunday).

For example, WEEKDAY("8/23/2016") returns 4 because August 23, 2017, is a Wednesday.

B5	▼	:	✕	✓	*fx*	=WEEKDAY($B$1)	

◢	A	B	C	D
1	Date:	August 23, 2017		
2	Year:	2017		
3	Month:	8		
4	Day:	23		
5	Weekday:	4		

The WEEKDAY function returns the day of the week for a specified date

Because Excel treats dates as serial numbers, you can calculate the difference between two dates by subtracting one date from another. However, the result includes weekends and holidays. In many business situations, you need to know the number of *workdays* between two dates. For example, when calculating the number of days an invoice is past due, it's often best to exclude weekends and holidays.

To calculate the serial number of the day that is a specified number of working days from a start date, with weekends and holidays excluded, use the WORKDAY function:

WORKDAY(start_date, days[, holidays])

E4	▼	:	✕	✓	*fx*	=WORKDAY(D4, 30)	

◢	A	B	C	D	E
3	Account Name	Account Number	Invoice Number	Invoice Date	Due Date
4	Around the Horn	10-0009	117321	January 19, 2017	Thursday, March 2, 2017
5	Around the Horn	10-0009	117327	February 1, 2017	Wednesday, March 15, 2017
6	Around the Horn	10-0009	117339	February 19, 2017	Friday, March 31, 2017
7	Around the Horn	10-0009	117344	March 5, 2017	Friday, April 14, 2017

The WORKDAY function returns the date that is a specified number of workdays past a starting date

To calculate the number of workdays between two dates, use the NETWORKDAYS function (read the name as "net workdays"):

NETWORKDAYS(start_date, end_date[, holidays])

The following table describes the WORKDAYS and NETWORKDAYS function arguments.

Argument	Description
start_date	The starting date (or a string representation of the date).
days	The number of workdays after *start_date*.
end_date	The ending date (or a string representation of the date).
holidays	A list of dates to exclude from the calculation. This can be a range of dates or an array constant—that is, a series of date serial numbers or date strings, separated by commas and surrounded by braces ({}).

H3	▼	:	✕	✓	*fx*	=NETWORKDAYS(E3, $H$1)

⬚	E	F	G	H
1			**Current Date:**	**April 25, 2017**
2	**Due Date**	**Invoice Amount**	**Date Paid**	**Days Overdue**
3	Thursday, March 2, 2017	$2,144.55		39
4	Wednesday, March 15, 2017	$1,847.25		30
5	Friday, March 31, 2017	$1,234.69	March 25, 2017	

The NETWORKDAYS function returns the number of workdays between two dates

A time consists of three components: the hour, minute, and second. It often happens that a worksheet generates one or more of these components, and you need some way of building a proper time out of them. You can do that by using the TIME function:

   TIME(hour, minute, second)

The following table describes the TIME function arguments.

Argument	Description
hour	The hour component of the time (a number from 0 through 23)
minute	The minute component of the time (a number from 0 through 59)
second	The second component of the time (a number from 0 through 59)

For example, TIME(14, 45, 30) returns the time 2:45:30 PM. Like the DATE function, TIME adjusts for wrong hour, minute, and second values. For example, TIME(14, 60, 30) returns 3:00:30 PM. Here, TIME takes the extra minute and adds 1 to the hour value.

The three components of a time—hour, minute, and second—can also be extracted individually from a specified time, by using the HOUR, MINUTE, and SECOND functions:

HOUR(serial_number)
MINUTE(serial_number)
SECOND(serial_number)

In each case, the *serial_number* argument is the time (or a string representation of the time) you want to work with. The HOUR function returns a number between 0 and 23 that corresponds to the hour component of a specified time. For example, HOUR(0.5) returns 12.

The MINUTE function returns a number between 0 and 59 that corresponds to the minute component of a specified time. For example, if it's currently 3:15 PM, MINUTE(NOW) returns 15.

The SECOND function returns a number between 0 and 59 that corresponds to the second component of a specified time. For example, SECOND("2:45:30 PM") returns 30.

B2	▼ ┊	✕ ✓ *fx*	=HOUR($B$1)
▲	A	B	C
1	Time:	2:45:30 PM	
2	Hour:	14	
3	Minute:	45	
4	Second:	30	

The HOUR, MINUTE, and SECOND functions return the individual components of a specified time

To insert a date or time function into a formula

→ On the **Formulas** tab, in the **Function Library** group, click **Date & Time**, click one of the date or time functions, and then enter the arguments, as described earlier in this chapter.

Objective 3.3 practice tasks

The practice file for these tasks is located in the **MOSExcelExpert2016 \Objective3** practice file folder. The folder also contains a result file that you can use to check your work.

➤ Open the **ExcelExpert_3-3** workbook and do the following:

❑ On the **Historical Events** worksheet, for each event listed, use the values in the year (column B), the month (column C), and the day (column D) in a formula to calculate the date on which each event occurs.

❑ On the **Dates** worksheet, in cells B2:B12, create formulas that return new dates that are one year, six months, and 15 days later than the dates in A2:A12.

❑ On the **Accounts Receivable Aging** worksheet, populate the Due Date column (D4:D14) with formulas that return dates that are 60 workdays after the dates in the Invoice Date column (C4:C14).

❑ On the same worksheet, add formulas to the Past Due column (E4:E14) that calculate the number of workdays that have elapsed between the Due Date value and the date shown in cell B1.

➤ Save the workbook.

➤ Open the **ExcelExpert_3-3_results** workbook. Compare the two workbooks to check your work, and then close the open workbooks.

Objective 3.4: Perform data analysis and business intelligence

It's often not enough to just enter data in a worksheet, build a few formulas, and add some formatting to make everything look presentable. In the business world, you're often called on to extract meaning from the jumble of numbers and formula results in your workbooks. In other words, you need to *analyze* your data to unearth conclusions, trends, and useful business knowledge. In Excel, going deeper into business data means using the program's data analysis and business intelligence tools.

Import, transform, combine, display, and connect to data

Get & Transform is a powerful Excel feature designed to provide you with easy and flexible connections to data in various formats, which you can then shape as needed by using queries. A *query* is a request to a data source for specific information. It combines criteria and extract conditions with functions to retrieve the data you want to work with. You can use Get & Transform to construct queries easily by using menu commands and drag-and-drop techniques. You can combine data from multiple sources, modify data types and formats to display the data the way you want, and then save the results to Excel. There are three main components to a Get & Transform operation:

- **Connect and import** This component involves making a connection to a data source, which could be on your PC, on your network, or in the cloud. You then select an item from that data source and import the data into Excel.

- **Transform** This component involves taking the raw data and shaping it so that you can view the data the way you want.

- **Combine** This optional component involves taking the transformed data from two or more sources and bringing them together in a unique or useful way.

Connect to and import data

The first step in using Get & Transform is to connect to a data source, which could be a file, such as a comma-separated text file; a database, such as a Microsoft Access database; or even a webpage table.

3

You choose which type of connection you want by clicking the New Query button in the Get & Transform group on the Data tab.

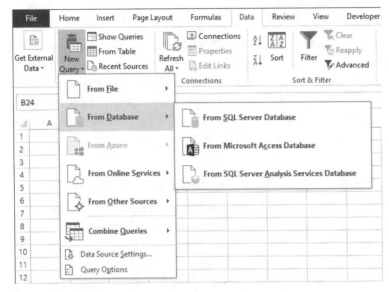

From the New Query menu, choose the type of connection you want to make

There are five main connection types on the New Query menu:

- **From File** This type includes individual files, such as Excel workbooks, comma-separated values (CSV) text files, extensible markup language (XML) files, other text files, and JavaScript Object Notation (JSON) files.

- **From Database** This type includes connections to database files or servers, including Microsoft Access, SQL Server, MySQL, and Oracle.

- **From Azure** This type includes data that resides on the Microsoft Azure cloud platform, including HDInsight and Blob Storage.

- **From Online Services** This type includes connections to online data sources, such as Facebook and Salesforce.com.

- **From Other Sources** This type includes webpages, Open Data Protocol (OData) feeds, and Open Database Connectivity (ODBC) sources.

IMPORTANT The data sources that appear on the New Query menu depend on your version of Excel. For example, users with an Office 365 ProPlus or Office 2016 Professional Plus license see more sources than those with a Home or Personal license.

How you connect to each varies depending on the data source type. In most cases, however, you see the Navigator dialog box, which you use to choose which item (or items) from the data source you want to import into Excel.

In the Navigator dialog box, you can preview a data source item before loading it into the query

To connect to and import external data

1. On the **Data** tab, in the **Get & Transform** group, click **New Query**, point to the type of data you want to import, and then in the submenu, click the data source type.

2. Enter the data source connection parameters. The specifics of this step vary depending on the data source.

3. Do either of the following to select the data:

   - If the **Navigator** dialog box appears, click any data source item to preview it in the dialog box. When you find the one you want to use, click it, and then click **Load** to import the data into the worksheet. To import two or more items from the data source, select the **Select Multiple Items** check box and then select the check box beside each item you want to import.

   - If the **Import Data** dialog box appears, select the file you want to use as the data source and then click **Open** to open the file in the Query Editor. You can either click **Close & Load** to import the data into Excel or leave the Query Editor open to transform the data, as described in the next section.

Transform data

After Excel imports the raw data into the worksheet, you will usually want to *transform* the data, which refers to modifying the data in a way that helps you analyze it. Example transforms include changing a column's data type, formatting column text, applying an arithmetic operation to a numeric column, and extracting a time from a date/time column. The idea is to form the data into a configuration that you can use to analyze the data within Excel, a process called *shaping* the data.

You transform data by using the commands on the Transform tab of the Query Editor.

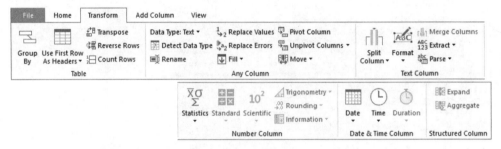

The available commands change based on the active data type.

There are five main ways that you can use the Query Editor to shape the data:

- **Entire table** You can group the table data by the values in a column, specify the first row as the table headers, transpose the rows and columns, reverse the order of the rows, or display a count of the rows.

- **Any column** For the selected column, you can change the data type, detect the data type, rename the column, replace one value for another throughout, replace errors with a specified value, fill empty cells with a specified value, pivot the table based on the unique values in the column, unpivot columns, and move the column left or right.

- **Text data** For a selected column that contains text, you can split the column based on a delimiter (such as a comma or space) or a specified number of characters; you can format the text by changing case, trimming blanks, removing non-printable characters, or applying a prefix or suffix; you can extract characters; and you can parse XML or JSON data. For two or more selected columns, you can merge the data into a single column.

- **Numeric data** For a selected column that contains numbers, you can apply statistics such as sum and average; you can transform the numbers by applying standard arithmetic operations such as addition and multiplication; you can apply scientific transforms such as raising the numbers to a power and taking the square root; you can apply trigonometric operations, such as the sine or cosine; you can round the numbers; and you can apply information transforms, such as showing whether the values are odd or even.

- **Date and time data** For a selected column that contains dates or times, you can *age* the data—that is, show the duration between the column value and the current date and time; display only the date or the time in columns that show both; return a specific date or time component, such as the year, month, or hour; show the earliest or latest date or time; and extract data from a duration column, such as the total number of years or days.

To load a query into the Query Editor

1. Click anywhere inside the query.

2. On the **Query** tool tab, in the **Edit** group, click **Edit**.

> **Tip** If you have the Workbook Queries pane open (on the Data tab, in the Get & Transform group, click Show Queries), you can also load a query into the Query Editor by double-clicking it.

To transform data

1. Load the query into the Query Editor.

2. To remove a column, click anywhere inside the column and then, on the **Home** tab, in the **Manage Columns** group, click **Remove Columns**.

3. To perform other transforms, select a column or columns, click the **Transform** tab, and then use the commands in the **Table**, **Any Column**, **Text Column**, **Number Column**, or **Date & Time Column** groups to apply your transforms.

4. On the **Home** tab, in the **Close** group, click **Close & Load** to return to Excel.

To remove a transform

1. Load the query into the Query Editor.

2. In the **Applied Steps** section of the **Query Settings** pane, point to the transform that you want to remove, and then click the **Delete** icon (**X**) that appears to the left of the transform.

Combine data

It is very common for multiple tables to be associated with each other in some way. This could mean that the tables have a common structure, or it could mean that the tables are related on a common field. As an example of the latter, a Suppliers table might have a SupplierID column that assigns a unique value to each supplier, whereas a Products table might use the same SupplierID column to reference the supplier of each product.

Depending on the nature of what the tables have in common, you can combine them in one of two ways:

- **Append** This operation adds one table to another based on the columns the tables have in common.

- **Merge** This operation brings two tables together based on the values in their related fields.

When merging tables, you must specify the related column in each table

To append data

1. Load the query into the Query Editor.

2. On the **Home** tab, in the **Combine** group, click **Append Queries** to open the Append dialog box.

3. Select the table you want to append to the current query, and then click **OK**.

4. On the **Home** tab, in the **Close** group, click **Close & Load** to return the appended data to Excel.

To merge data

1. Load the query into the Query Editor.

2. On the **Home** tab, in the **Combine** group, click **Merge Queries** to open the Merge dialog box.

3. Select the table you want to merge with the current query.

4. For each table, click the header of the field by which the two tables are related.

5. Click **OK**.

6. On the **Home** tab, in the **Close** group, click **Close & Load** to return the merged data to Excel.

Consolidate data

Many businesses create worksheets for specific tasks and then distribute them to various departments. The most common example is budgeting. Accounting might create a generic "budget" template that each department or division in the company must fill out and return. Similarly, you often see worksheets distributed for inventory requirements, sales forecasting, survey data, experimental results, and more.

Creating these worksheets, distributing them, and filling them in are all straightforward operations. However, the tricky part comes when the sheets are returned to the originating department, and all the new data must be combined into a summary report showing companywide totals. This task is called *consolidating* the data, and it's often complicated and time consuming, especially for large worksheets. Fortunately, Excel has powerful features that can take the drudgery out of consolidation.

3

Excel can consolidate your data by using the following methods:

- **Consolidating by position** With this method, Excel consolidates the data from several worksheets, using the same range coordinates on each sheet. You can use this method if the worksheets you're consolidating have an identical layout.

- **Consolidating by category** This method tells Excel to consolidate the data by looking for identical row and column labels in each sheet. For example, if one worksheet lists monthly Gizmo sales in row 1 and another lists monthly Gizmo sales in row 5, you can consolidate this information as long as both sheets have a "Gizmo" label at the beginning of these rows.

In both cases, you specify one or more *source ranges* (the ranges that contain the data you want to consolidate) and a *destination range* (the range where the consolidated data will appear).

If the sheets you're working with have the same layout, consolidating by position is the easiest way to go. For example, consider three workbooks—Division I Budget, Division II Budget, and Division III Budget. Each sheet uses the same row and column labels, so they're ideal candidates for consolidation by position.

During the consolidation procedure, Excel defaults to creating links to the source data, which means it updates the consolidated data when the source data changes. To make this happen, Excel does three things:

- It adds link formulas to the destination range for each cell in the source ranges you selected.

- It consolidates the data by adding SUM functions (or whichever operation you select) that total the results of the link formulas.

- It outlines the consolidation worksheet and hides the link formulas.

When your worksheets are laid out identically, consolidate them by position

If you want to consolidate data from worksheets that don't use the same layout, you need to tell Excel to consolidate the data by category. In this case, Excel examines each of your source ranges and consolidates data that uses the same row or column labels.

To consolidate data by position

1. Create a new worksheet that has the same layout as the sheets you're consolidating.

2. In this new consolidation worksheet, click the upper-left corner of the destination range.

3. On the **Data** tab, in the **Data Tools** group, click **Consolidate** to open the Consolidate dialog box.

4. In the **Function** list, click the operation to use during the consolidation. You'll use Sum most of the time, but Excel has 10 other operations to choose from, including Count, Average, Max, and Min.

5. For each source range—not including any row and/or column labels—enter the range coordinates in the **Reference** box, and then click **Add**. If the source data is open in another worksheet or workbook, you can click the range box and then select the data.

6. If you want the consolidated data to change whenever you make changes to the source data, make sure that the **Create links to source data** check box is selected.

7. Click **OK**. Excel gathers the data, consolidates it, and then adds it to the destination range.

To consolidate data by category

1. Create or select a new worksheet and click the upper-left corner of the destination range.

> **IMPORTANT** When consolidating by category, it isn't necessary to enter labels for the consolidated data because Excel does it for you automatically. If you want to see the labels in a particular order, it's okay to enter them yourself. However, if you do enter the labels yourself, make sure you spell the labels exactly as they're spelled in the source worksheets.

2. On the **Data** tab, in the **Data Tools** group, click **Consolidate** to open the Consolidate dialog box.

3. In the **Function** list, click the operation to use during the consolidation.

4. For each source range—including any row and/or column labels—enter the range coordinates in the **Reference** box, and then click **Add**. If the source data is open in another worksheet or workbook, you can click the range box and then select the data.

5. If you want Excel to use the data labels in the top row of the selected ranges, under **Use labels in**, select the **Top row** check box. If you want Excel to use the data labels in the left column of the source ranges, select the **Left column** check box.

6. If you want the consolidated data to change whenever you make changes to the source data, make sure that the **Create links to source data** check box is selected.

7. Click **OK**. Excel gathers the data, consolidates it, and then adds it to the destination range.

Perform what-if analysis by using Goal Seek and Scenario Manager

What-if analysis is perhaps the most basic method for interrogating your worksheet data. With what-if analysis, you first calculate a formula, D, based on the input from variables A, B, and C. You then say, "What if I change variable A? Or B or C? What happens to the result?"

Perform what-if analysis by using Goal Seek

Here's a what-if question for you: What if you already know the result you want? For example, you might know that you want to have $50,000 saved to purchase new equipment five years from now, or that you have to achieve a 30% gross margin in your next budget. If you need to manipulate only a single variable to achieve these results, you can use the Goal Seek feature in Excel. You tell Goal Seek the final value you need and which variable to change, and it finds a solution for you (if one exists).

When you set up a worksheet to use Goal Seek, you usually have a formula in one cell and the formula's variable—with an initial value—in another. (Your formula can have multiple variables, but with Goal Seek you can manipulate only one variable at a time.) Goal Seek operates by using an *iterative method* to find a solution. That is, Goal Seek first tries the variable's initial value to see whether that produces the result you want. If it doesn't, Goal Seek tries different values until it converges on a solution.

Before you run Goal Seek, you need to set up your worksheet in a particular way. This means doing three things:

- Set up one cell as the *changing cell*. This is the value that Goal Seek will iteratively manipulate to attempt to reach the goal. Enter an initial value (such as 0) into the cell.

- Set up the other input values for the formula and make them proper initial values.

- Create a formula for Goal Seek to use to try to reach the goal.

For example, suppose you're a small-business owner looking to purchase new equipment worth $50,000 five years from now. Assuming your investments earn 5 percent annual interest, how much do you need to set aside every year to reach this goal? You can set up a worksheet like this to use Goal Seek:

- Make cell C5 the changing cell: the annual deposit into the fund (with an initial value of 0).

- In cells C3 and C4, enter the constants for the FV function.

- Make cell C7 the cell that contains the FV function that calculates the future value of the equipment fund. When Goal Seek is done, this cell's value should be $50,000.

C7	▼	:	✕	✓	*fx*	=FV(C3, C4, C5)

⊿	A	B	C	D
1		*Equipment Fund Calculation*		
2				
3		**Interest Rate**	5%	
4		**Period**	5	
5		**Annual Deposit**	$0	
6				
7		**Equipment Fund**	$0	

A worksheet set up to use Goal Seek to find out how much to set aside each year to end up with a $50,000 equipment fund in five years

To perform what-if analysis by using Goal Seek

1. On the **Data** tab, in the **Forecast** group, click **What-If Analysis**, and then click **Goal Seek** to open the Goal Seek dialog box.

2. In the **Set cell** box, enter a reference to the cell that contains the formula you want Goal Seek to manipulate.

3. In the **To value** box, enter the final value you want for the goal cell.

4. In the **By changing cell** box, enter a reference to the changing cell.

Goal Seek	?	×
Set cell:	C7	
To value:	50000	
By changing cell:	$C$5	
	OK	Cancel

The Goal Seek dialog box configured to perform analysis

5. Click **OK**. Excel begins the iteration and displays the Goal Seek Status dialog box. When Excel finishes, the dialog box tells you whether Goal Seek found a solution.

6. If Goal Seek found a solution, you can accept the solution by clicking **OK**. To ignore the solution, click **Cancel**.

		Goal Seek Status	?	×
Interest Rate	5%	Goal Seeking with Cell C7	Step	
Period	5	found a solution.		
Annual Deposit	($9,049)	Target value: 50000	Pause	
		Current value: $50,000		
Equipment Fund	$50,000		OK	Cancel

Goal Seek lets you know whether it found a solution

Perform what-if analysis by using Scenario Manager

By definition, what-if analysis is not an exact science. All what-if models make guesses and assumptions based on history, expected events, and other factors. A particular set of guesses and assumptions that you plug into a model is called a *scenario*. Because most what-if worksheets can take a wide range of input values, you usually end up with a large number of scenarios to examine. Instead of going through the tedious chore of inserting all these values into the appropriate cells, Excel has a Scenario Manager feature that can handle the process for you.

As an example, imagine a worksheet model that analyzes a mortgage. You'd use such a model to decide how much of a down payment to make, how long the term should be, and whether to include an extra principal paydown every month.

=PMT(Interest_Rate / 12, Term * 12, House_Price - Down_Payment)

B	C	D
Mortgage Analysis		
Fixed Cells:		
House Price	$100,000	
Interest Rate	4.00%	
Changing Cells:		
Down Payment	$20,000	
Term	20	
Paydown	($100)	
Results:	**Regular Mortgage**	**With Paydown**
Monthly Payment	($484.78)	($584.78)
Total Paid	($116,348.22)	($106,986.75)
Total Savings	#N/A	$9,361.47
Revised Term	#N/A	15.2

A worksheet model set up to analyze a mortgage

Here are some possible questions to ask this model:

- How much will I save over the term of the mortgage if I use a shorter term, make a larger down payment, and include a monthly paydown?

- How much more will I end up paying if I extend the term, reduce the down payment, and forgo the paydown?

These are examples of scenarios that you would plug into the appropriate cells in the model. Scenario Manager helps by letting you define a scenario separately from the worksheet. You can save specific values for any or all of the model's input cells, give the scenario a name, and then recall the name (and all the input values it contains) from a list.

Before creating a scenario, you need to decide which cells in your model will be the input cells. These will be the worksheet variables—the cells that, when you change them, change the results of the model. Excel calls these the *changing cells*. You can have as many as 32 changing cells in a scenario. For best results, follow these guidelines when setting up your worksheet for scenarios:

- The changing cells should be constants. Formulas can be affected by other cells, and that can throw off the entire scenario.

- To make it easier to set up each scenario, and to make your worksheet easier to understand, group the changing cells and label them.

- For even greater clarity, assign a name to each changing cell.

To add a scenario

1. On the **Data** tab, in the **Forecast** group, click **What-If Analysis**, and then click **Scenario Manager** to open the Scenario Manager dialog box.

2. Click **Add** to open the Add Scenario dialog box.

3. In the **Scenario name** box, enter a name for the scenario.

4. In the **Changing cells** box, enter references to your worksheet's changing cells. You can type in the references (be sure to separate noncontiguous cells with commas) or select the cells directly on the worksheet.

5. In the **Comment** box, enter a description for the scenario. This description appears in the Comment section of the Scenario Manager dialog box.

6. Click **OK**. Excel opens the Scenario Values dialog box.

7. In the **Scenario Values** dialog box, enter values for the changing cells.

8. To add more scenarios, click **Add** to return to the Add Scenario dialog box and repeat steps 3 through 7. Otherwise, click **OK** to return to the Scenario Manager dialog box.

9. Click **Close** to save the scenario and return to the worksheet.

To display a scenario

1. On the **Data** tab, in the **Forecast** group, click **What-If Analysis**, and then click **Scenario Manager** to open the Scenario Manager dialog box.

2. In the **Scenarios** list, click the scenario you want to display.

3. Click **Show**. Excel enters the scenario values into the changing cells.

4. Repeat steps 2 and 3 to display other scenarios.

5. Click **Close** to return to the worksheet.

Use cube functions to get data out of the Excel data model

In the business world, it is common to work with data sources that contain anywhere from hundreds of thousands of records to millions, even billions, of records. You cannot place such a huge data source on a worksheet, and even trying to manipulate all that data via a regular external data source is extremely time-consuming and resource-intensive. Fortunately, such huge data sources often reside on special servers that use a technology called *Online Analytical Processing*, or *OLAP*. By using OLAP, you can retrieve and summarize immense and complex data sources. When combined with Excel, OLAP enables you to view the data in a PivotTable or PivotChart report, or manipulate the data with Power Pivot, quickly and easily.

In a traditional relational database management system, or RDBMS, such as Access, multiple tables are related by using common fields. In the Northwind sample database, for example, the Customers table is related to the Orders table based on the common Customer ID field, and the Orders table is related to the Order Details table on the common Order ID field. You can use a query to pick and choose fields from each table and return them in a dataset. However, this can be a very slow process in a massive data source, so OLAP uses a different concept called the *data warehouse*. This is a data structure—called a *star schema*—with a central fact table that contains the numeric data you want to summarize and pointers to surrounding related tables.

A *fact table* is the primary table in a data warehouse. It contains data about events or processes—the facts—within a business, such as sales transactions or company expenses. Each record in the fact table contains two types of data: measures and dimensions.

A *measure* is a column of numeric values within the fact table. It represents the data that you want to summarize. In a data warehouse of sales transactions, for example, there might be one measure for units sold and another for dollars earned. An OLAP measure is analogous to a data field in a regular data source.

A *dimension* is a category of data, so it is analogous to a row, column, or report filter in an ordinary data source. However, dimensions often contain hierarchical groupings called *levels*. For example, a Store dimension might have a hierarchy of location levels, such as Country, State, and City. Similarly, a Time dimension might have Year, Quarter, and Month levels. Each level has its own set of items, called *members*. For example, the Month level has the items January, February, and so on. Because most fact tables contain keys to multiple dimension tables, OLAP data is often called *multidimensional data*.

An *OLAP cube*—or simply a *cube*—is a data structure that takes the information in a data warehouse and summarizes each measure by every dimension, level, and member. For example, a three-dimensional cube might summarize sales based on the dimensions of Time, Product, and Store. The cube could then tell you, for example, the units sold of rye bread at store #6 in January, or the dollars' worth of scissors sold in California in the second quarter. All of the measures are precalculated in the cube, so Excel does not have to perform any calculations when you use a cube as a data source.

However, there might be times when you need to extract data from the cube for use outside of Power Pivot or a PivotTable. For example, you might want to highlight a key calculation in a summary worksheet. To extract data in this way, you can use cube functions, which are designed to work with cube data contained in an Excel data model.

=CUBEVALUE("ThisWorkbookDataModel","[Measures].[Sum of SalesQuantity]", "[ProductName].[SV Keyboard E10 Black]", "[ChannelName].[Online]")

B	C	D
Key Metrics:		
Online Unit Sales of the E10 Keyboard	4,363	
Total Units Sold	53,320,454	
Average Sales Per Transaction	$3,112.93	

You can use cube functions such as CUBEVALUE to extract data from a cube

The following cube functions are available:

- **CUBEKPIMEMBER** Returns a key performance indicator (KPI) property and displays the KPI name in the cell. A KPI is a quantifiable measurement, such as monthly gross profit or quarterly employee turnover, that is used to monitor an organization's performance. Here's the syntax:

  CUBEKPIMEMBER(connection, kpi_name, kpi_property[, caption])

- **CUBEMEMBER** Returns a member from the cube, which you can use to validate that the member exists in the cube. Here's the syntax:

  CUBEMEMBER(connection, member_expression[, caption])

- **CUBEMEMBERPROPERTY** Returns the value of a member property from the cube, which you can use to validate that a member name exists within the cube and to return the specified property for this member. Here's the syntax:

  CUBEMEMBERPROPERTY(connection, member_expression, property)

- **CUBERANKEDMEMBER** Returns the *n*th, or ranked, member in a set. Use this function to return one or more elements in a set, such as the top sales performer or the top 10 students. Here's the syntax:

  CUBERANKEDMEMBER(connection, set_expression, rank[, caption])

  To return the top five values, use CUBERANKEDMEMBER five times, specifying a different rank, 1 through 5, each time.

- **CUBESET** Defines a calculated set of members by sending a set expression to the cube on the server, which creates the set, and then returns that set to Excel. Here's the syntax:

  CUBESET(connection, set_expression[, caption][, sort_order][, sort_by])

- **CUBESETCOUNT** Returns the number of items in a set. Here's the syntax:

  CUBESETCOUNT(set)

- **CUBEVALUE** Returns an aggregated value from the cube. Here's the syntax:

  CUBEVALUE(connection[, member_expression1][, member_expression2, ...])

The following table describes the arguments for the cube functions

Argument	Description
caption	A text string that is displayed in the cell instead of the caption, if one is defined, from the cube.
	For the CUBEKPIMEMBER function, alternative text that is displayed in the cell instead of *kpi_name* and *kpi_property*.
connection	A text string specifying the name of the connection to the cube.
kpi_name	A text string specifying the name of the KPI in the cube.
kpi_property	The KPI component returned. This can be one of the following:

Integer	Enumerated constant	Description
1	KPIValue	The actual value
2	KPIGoal	A target value
3	KPIStatus	The state of the KPI at a specific moment in time
4	KPITrend	A measure of the value over time
5	KPIWeight	A relative importance assigned to the KPI
6	KPICurrentTimeMember	A temporal context for the KPI

Argument	Description
member_expression	Defines the portion of the cube for which the aggregated value is returned. Can be either of the following:
	▪ A multidimensional expression that specifies a member within the cube.
	▪ A set defined with the CUBESET function.
	If no measure is specified in *member_expression*, the function uses the default measure for that cube.
property	A text string of the name of the property returned or a reference to a cell that contains the name of the property.
rank	An integer value specifying the top value to return. If *rank* is a value of 1, it returns the top value; if *rank* is a value of 2, it returns the value second from the top; and so on.
set	Any of the following:
	▪ An expression that evaluates to a set defined by the CUBESET function
	▪ The CUBESET function
	▪ A reference to a cell that contains the CUBESET function

3

Argument	Description
set_expression	Any of the following: • A text string of a set expression, such as "{[Item1].children}", that results in a set of members • A cell reference to an Excel range that contains one or more members or sets included in the set • The CUBESET function • A reference to a cell or cell range that contains the CUBESET function
sort_by	The name of the member on which you want to sort the results.
sort_order	The type of sort, if any, to perform. Options include:

Integer	Description	sort_by argument
0	Leaves the set in existing order	Ignored
1	Sorts set in ascending order by sort_by	Required
2	Sorts set in descending order by sort_by	Required
3	Sorts set in alpha ascending order	Ignored
4	Sorts set in alpha descending order	Ignored
5	Sorts set in natural ascending order	Ignored
6	Sorts set in natural descending order	Ignored

To insert a cube function into a formula

→ On the **Formulas** tab, in the **Function Library** group, click **More Functions**, point to **Cube**, click the cube function you want to use, and then enter the arguments, as described earlier in this chapter.

Calculate data by using financial functions

Excel is loaded with financial features that give you powerful tools for building models that manage both business and personal finances. You can use these functions to calculate such things as the monthly payment on a loan, the future value of an annuity, the internal rate of return of an investment, or the yearly depreciation of an asset.

Most of the formulas you'll work with involve three factors—the *present value* (the amount something is worth now); the *future value* (the amount something will be worth in the future); and the interest rate (or the discount rate)—plus two related factors: the *periods*, the number of payments or deposits over the term of the loan or investment, and the *payment*, the amount of money paid out or invested in each period.

Although Excel has dozens of financial functions that use many different arguments, the following table describes the arguments you'll use most frequently.

Argument	Description
rate	The fixed rate of interest over the term of the loan or investment.
nper	The number of payments or deposit periods over the term of the loan or investment.
pmt	The periodic payment or deposit.
pv	The present value of the loan (the principal) or the initial deposit in an investment.
fv	The future value of the loan or investment.
type	The type of payment or deposit. Use 0 (the default) for end-of-period payments or deposits, and 1 for beginning-of-period payments or deposits.

When building financial formulas, you need to ask yourself the following questions:

- **Who or what is the subject of the formula?** On a mortgage analysis, for example, are you performing the analysis on behalf of yourself or the bank?

- **Which way is the money flowing with respect to the subject?** For the present value, future value, and payment, enter money that the subject receives as a positive quantity, and enter money that the subject pays out as a negative quantity. For example, if you're the subject of a mortgage analysis, the loan principal (the present value) is a positive number because it's money that you receive from the bank; the payment and the remaining principal (the future value) are negative because they're amounts that you pay to the bank.

- **What is the time unit?** The underlying unit of both the interest rate and the period must be the same. For example, if you're working with the annual interest rate, you must express the period in years. Similarly, if you're working with monthly periods, you must use a monthly interest rate.

3

- **When are the payments made?** Excel differentiates between payments made at the end of each period and those made at the beginning.

=PMT(C2 / 12, C3 * 12, C4, -C5)

B	C
Loan Payment Analysis	
Interest Rate (Annual)	6.00%
Periods (Years)	5
Principal	$10,000
Balloon Payment	$3,000
Monthly Payment	($150.33)

Using the PMT function to calculate a loan payment

The following table shows the most commonly used financial functions.

Function	Returns
CUMIPMT(*rate, nper, pv, start, end, type*)	The cumulative interest paid on a loan between *start* and *end*
CUMPRINC(*rate, nper, pv, start, end, type*)	The cumulative principal paid on a loan between *start* and *end*
DB(*cost, salvage, life, period, month*)	The depreciation of an asset over a specified period using the fixed-declining balance method
DDB(*cost, salvage, life, period, factor*)	The depreciation of an asset over a specified period using the double-declining balance method
EFFECT(*nominal_rate, npery*)	The effective annual interest rate given the nominal annual interest rate and the number of yearly compounding periods
FV(*rate, nper, pmt, pv, type*)	The future value of an investment or loan
IPMT(*rate, per, nper, pv, fv, type*)	The interest payment for a specified period of a loan
IRR(*values, guess*)	The internal rate of return for a series of cash flows
MIRR(*values, finance_rate, reinvest_rate*)	The modified internal rate of return for a series of periodic cash flows

Function	Returns
NOMINAL(*effect_rate*, *npery*)	The nominal annual interest rate given the effective annual interest rate and the number of yearly compounding periods
NPER(*rate*, *pmt*, *pv*, *fv*, *type*)	The number of periods for an investment or loan based on fixed payments and interest rate
NPV(*rate*, *value1*, *value2...*)	The net present value of an investment based on a series of cash flows and a discount rate
PMT(*rate*, *nper*, *pv*, *fv*, *type*)	The periodic payment for a loan or investment
PPMT(*rate*, *per*, *nper*, *pv*, *fv*, *type*)	The principal payment for a specified period of a loan
PV(*rate*, *nper*, *pmt*, *fv*, *type*)	The present value of an investment
RATE(*nper*, *pmt*, *pv*, *fv*, *type*, *guess*)	The periodic interest rate for a loan or investment
SLN(*cost*, *salvage*, *life*)	The straight-line depreciation of an asset over one period
SYD(*cost*, *salvage*, *life*, *period*)	The sum-of-years' digits depreciation of an asset over a specified period

3

To insert a financial function into a formula

→ On the **Formulas** tab, in the **Function Library** group, click **Financial**, click the financial function you want to use, and then enter the arguments, as described earlier in this chapter.

Objective 3.4 practice tasks

The practice files for these tasks are located in the **MOSExcelExpert2016 \Objective3** practice file folder. The folder also contains a result file that you can use to check your work.

➤ Open the **ExcelExpert_3-4** workbook and do the following:

❑ Create a query based on the **ExcelExpert_3-4_CSV.csv** file.

❑ Load the query into the workbook.

➤ Open the Query Editor and do the following:

❑ Split the Contact Name column based on the rightmost occurrence of the space character.

❑ Create a new column named Invoice Total that displays the sum of the Extended Price column and the Freight column.

❑ Return the transformed data to Excel and rename the new worksheet as Invoices.

❑ On the **Consolidate by Position** worksheet, consolidate the data from the **ExcelExpert_3-4a**, **ExcelExpert_3-4b**, and **ExcelExpert_3-4c** workbooks.

❑ On the **Consolidate by Category** worksheet, consolidate the data from the **ExcelExpert_3-4d**, **ExcelExpert_3-4e**, and **ExcelExpert_3-4f** workbooks.

❑ On the **Break Even** worksheet, use Goal Seek to determine the number of units that must be sold to break even (that is, generate a profit equal to 0).

❑ On the **Scenarios** worksheet, create three scenarios for the model: Best Case ($20,000 down payment, 20-year term, and $100 paydown); Worst Case ($10,000 down payment, 30-year term, and $0 paydown); and Likeliest Case ($15,000 down payment, 25-year term, and $50 paydown).

➤ Save the **ExcelExpert_3-4** workbook.

➤ Open the **ExcelExpert_3-4_results** workbook. Compare the two workbooks to check your work, and then close the open workbooks.

Objective 3.5: Troubleshoot formulas

Despite your best efforts, an error might appear in your formulas from time to time. Such errors can be mathematical (for example, dividing by zero), or Excel might simply be incapable of interpreting the formula. In the latter case, problems can be caught while you're entering the formula. For example, if you try to enter a formula that has unbalanced parentheses, Excel won't accept the entry, and it displays an error message. Other errors are more insidious. For example, your formula might appear to be working—that is, it might return a value—but the result might be incorrect because the data is flawed or because your formula has referenced the wrong cell or range. Whatever the error and whatever the cause, formula woes need to be worked out because you or someone else in your company is likely depending on your models to produce accurate results.

Trace precedence and dependence

Some formula errors result from referencing other cells that contain errors or inappropriate values. The first step in troubleshooting these kinds of formula problems is to determine which cell (or group of cells) is causing an error. This is straightforward if the formula references only a single cell, but it gets progressively more difficult as the number of references increases. (Another complicating factor is the use of range names, because it won't be obvious which range each name is referencing.)

To determine which cells are wreaking havoc on your formulas, you can use Excel auditing features to visualize and trace a formula's input values and error sources. The formula-auditing features operate by creating tracers—arrows that literally point out the cells involved in a formula. You can use tracers to find two kinds of cells:

- **Precedents** These are cells that are directly or indirectly referenced in a formula. For example, suppose that cell E4 contains the formula =E2; E2 is a direct precedent of E4. Now suppose that cell E2 contains the formula =D2/2; this makes D2 a direct precedent of E2 and also an indirect precedent of cell E4.

- **Dependents** These are cells that are directly or indirectly referenced by a formula in another cell. In the preceding example, cell E2 is a direct dependent of D2, and E4 is an indirect dependent of D2.

Tracer arrows show the precedents of cell E4

To trace cell precedents

1. Select the cell that contains the formula whose precedents you want to trace.

2. On the **Formulas** tab, in the **Formula Auditing** group, click **Trace Precedents**. Excel adds a tracer arrow to each direct precedent.

3. Repeat step 2 to trace more levels of precedents.

Tip You also can trace precedents by double-clicking the cell, if you have turned off in-cell editing. You do this by clearing the Allow Editing Directly In Cells check box on the Advanced page of the Excel Options dialog box.

To trace cell dependents

1. Select the cell whose dependents you want to trace.

2. On the **Formulas** tab, in the **Formula Auditing** group, click **Trace Dependents**. Excel adds a tracer arrow to each direct dependent.

3. Repeat step 2 to trace more levels of dependents.

Monitor cells and formulas by using the Watch Window

It is very common for a formula to refer to a precedent that resides in a different worksheet. That's a powerful technique, but it does mean that you might not be able to see the formula cell and the precedent cell at the same time. This could also happen if the precedent exists in another workbook or even elsewhere on the same sheet, if you're working with a large model.

This is a problem because there's no easy way to determine the current value or formula of the unseen precedent. If you're having a problem, troubleshooting requires that you track down the far-off precedent to see if it might be the culprit. That's bad enough with a single unseen cell, but what if your formula refers to 5 or 10 such cells? And what if those cells are scattered in different worksheets and workbooks?

This level of hassle—not at all uncommon in the spreadsheet world—was no doubt the inspiration behind an elegant solution: the Watch Window. You use this window to keep track of both the value and the formula in any cell in any worksheet in any open workbook.

Use the Watch Window to keep track of the value or formula of a cell in any worksheet or workbook

To add a watch

1. Go to the workbook or worksheet that contains the cell or cells you want to watch.

2. On the **Formulas** tab, in the **Formula Auditing** group, click **Watch Window** to open the Watch Window.

3. Click **Add Watch** to open the Add Watch dialog box.

4. Do either of the following:

   • In the worksheet, select the cell or cell range you want to watch.

   • In the **Select the cells that you would like to watch the value of** box, enter a reference formula for the cell or cell range (for example, =A1).

5. Click **Add** to add the cell or cells to the Watch Window.

To remove a watch

1. On the **Formulas** tab, in the **Formula Auditing** group, click **Watch Window** to open the Watch Window.

2. Click the watch you want to remove.

3. Click **Delete Watch**. Excel removes the watch.

Validate formulas by using error-checking rules

If you use Microsoft Word, you're probably familiar with the wavy blue lines that appear under words and phrases that the grammar checker has flagged as being incorrect. The grammar checker operates by using a set of rules that determine correct grammar and syntax. As you type, the grammar checker operates in the background, constantly monitoring your writing. If something you write goes against one of the grammar checker's rules, the wavy line appears to let you know there's a problem.

Excel has a similar feature: the formula error checker. Like the grammar checker, the formula error checker uses a set of rules to determine correctness, and it operates in the background to monitor your formulas. If it detects something amiss, it displays an *error indicator*—a green triangle—in the upper-left corner of the cell containing the formula. When you select the cell with the formula error, Excel displays an icon beside the cell. If you point to the icon, a ScreenTip describes the error.

f_x	=F1 / (1 - F2)						
D	E	F	G	H	I	J	K
Final Price	$10.65	$21.35	$32.05				
Sales Tax	7%	7%	7%				
List Price	$ ⚡ ▾	$22.96	$29.95				

The formula in this cell differs from the formulas in this area of the spreadsheet.

Select the cell containing the error, and then point to the icon to see a description of the error

Clicking the icon displays the following options:

- **Corrective actions** One or more commands (depending on the type of error) that Excel suggests for either fixing the problem or helping you troubleshoot the error.

- **Help on this error** Click this option to get information on the error from the Excel Help system.

- **Ignore Error** Click this option to leave the formula as is.

- **Edit in Formula Bar** Click this option to display the formula in Edit mode in the formula bar. You can then fix the problem by editing the formula.

- **Error Checking Options** Click this option to display the Formulas page of the Excel Options dialog box (discussed next).

Like the Word grammar checker, the Excel formula error checker has several rules that control which errors it flags. You can configure these rules on the Formulas page of the Excel Options dialog box. The following list describes each rule, including the errors each rule flags and some of the corrective actions that Excel makes available on the error-checking menu that appears when you click the error icon next to a flagged cell:

- **Cells containing formulas that result in an error** Flags formulas that evaluate to an error value such as #DIV/0! or #NAME?.

- **Inconsistent calculated column formula in tables** In calculated columns, flags any cell that contains a formula with a different structure than the other cells in the column. The error-checking menu for this error includes the Restore To Calculated Column Formula command, which you can use to update the formula so that it's consistent with the rest of the column.

- **Cells containing years represented as 2 digits** Flags formulas that contain date text strings in which the year contains only two digits (a possibly ambiguous situation because the string could refer to a date in either the 1900s or the 2000s). The error-checking menu includes two commands—Convert XX To 19XX and Convert XX To 20XX—that you can use to convert the two-digit year to a four-digit year.

- **Numbers formatted as text or preceded by an apostrophe** Flags cells that contain a number that is either formatted as text or preceded by an apostrophe. The error-checking menu includes the Convert To Number command to convert the text to its numeric equivalent.

- **Formulas inconsistent with other formulas in the region** Flags formulas that are structured differently from similar formulas in the surrounding area. The error-checking menu includes a command such as Copy Formula From Left to bring the formula into consistency with the surrounding cells.

- **Formulas which omit cells in a region** Flags formulas that omit cells that are adjacent to a range referenced in the formula. For example, suppose that the formula is =AVERAGE(C4:C21), where C4:C21 is a range of numeric values. If cell C3 also contains a numeric value, the formula error checker flags the formula to alert you to the possibility that you missed including cell C3 in the formula.

- **Unlocked cells containing formulas** Flags formulas that reside in unlocked cells. This isn't an error so much as a warning that other people could tamper with the formula even after you have protected the sheet. The error-checking menu includes the command Lock Cell to lock the cell and prevent users from changing the formula after you protect the sheet.

- **Formulas referring to empty cells** Flags formulas that reference empty cells. The error-checking menu includes the Trace Empty Cell command to help you find the empty cell. (At this point, you can either enter data into the cell or adjust the formula so that it doesn't reference the cell.)

- **Data entered in a table is invalid** Flags cells that violate a table's data-validation rules. This can happen if you set up a data-validation rule with only a Warning or Information style, in which case the user can still opt to enter the invalid data. The formula error checker flags the cells that contain invalid data. The error-checking menu includes the Display Type Information command, which shows the data-validation rule that the cell data violates.

To configure the error-checking rules

→ On the **Formulas** page of the **Excel Options** dialog box, in the **Error checking rules** section, select or clear the check boxes to choose the rules you want to apply. Then click **OK**.

Tip You can display the Formulas page directly by clicking a cell containing an error, clicking the error checker icon, and then clicking Error Checking Options.

Evaluate formulas

If a formula produces no warnings or error values, the result might still be in error. If the result of a formula is incorrect, one method that can help you understand and fix the problem is to calculate multipart formulas one term at a time. In the formula bar, select the expression you want to calculate, and then press F9. Excel converts the expression into its value. Make sure that you press the Esc key when you're done, to avoid entering the formula with just the calculated values.

This is a useful technique, but it can be tedious in a long or complex formula, and there's always a danger that you might accidentally confirm a partially evaluated formula and lose your work. For complex formulas, a better solution is to use the Evaluate Formula feature in Excel. It does the same thing as the F9 technique, but it's easier and safer.

To evaluate a formula

1. Select the cell that contains the formula you want to evaluate.

2. On the **Formulas** tab, in the **Formula Auditing** group, click **Evaluate Formula** to open the Evaluate Formula dialog box.

3. The current term in the formula is underlined in the Evaluation box. At each step, select from one or more of the following buttons:

   - **Evaluate** Click this button to display the current value of the underlined term.

   - **Step In** Click this button to display the first dependent of the underlined term. If that dependent also has a dependent, click this button again to see it.

   - **Step Out** Click this button to hide a dependent and evaluate its precedent.

4. Repeat step 3 until you've completed your evaluation, and then click **Close**.

3

Objective 3.5 practice tasks

The practice file for these tasks is located in the **MOSExcelExpert2016 \Objective3** practice file folder. The folder also contains a result file that you can use to check your work.

➤ Open the **ExcelExpert_3-5** workbook, display the **Gross Margin** worksheet, and do the following:

❑ Trace the precedents of cell E4.

❑ Trace the dependents of cell G2.

➤ Display the **List Price** worksheet and do the following:

❑ Set up a watch for cell F4.

❑ Use the error checker to locate and fix the formula error on the worksheet.

➤ Return to the **Gross Margin** worksheet and do the following:

❑ Evaluate the formula in cell G4 by stepping into each of its components.

➤ Save the workbook.

➤ Open the **ExcelExpert_3-5_results** workbook. Compare the two workbooks to check your work, and then close the open workbooks.

Objective 3.6: Define named ranges and objects

Although you can use ranges to work efficiently with large groups of cells, there are some disadvantages to using range coordinates:

- Each time you want to use a range, you must check to see whether it still has the same coordinates (for example, one or more cells might have been inserted or deleted) and, if not, redefine its coordinates.

- Range notation is not intuitive. To know what a formula such as =SUM(E6:E10) is adding, you have to look at the range itself.

- A slight mistake in defining the range coordinates can lead to disastrous results, especially when you're erasing a range.

You can overcome these problems by using range names, which are labels applied to a single cell or to a range of cells. You can use a defined name in place of the range coordinates. For example, to include the range in a formula or range command, you use the name instead of selecting the range or entering its coordinates. You can create as many range names as you want, and you can even assign multiple names to the same range.

Range names also make your formulas intuitive and easy to read. For example, assigning the name AugustSales to a range such as E6:E10 immediately clarifies the purpose of a formula such as =SUM(AugustSales). Range names also increase the accuracy of your range operations because you don't have to specify range coordinates.

Besides overcoming these problems, range names offer several other advantages:

- Names are easier to remember than range coordinates.

- Names don't change when you move a range to another part of the worksheet.

- Named ranges adjust automatically whenever you insert or delete rows or columns within the range.

- Names make it easier to navigate a worksheet. You can use the Go To command to jump to a named range quickly.

- You can use worksheet labels to create range names quickly.

Range names can be quite flexible, but you need to keep in mind a few restrictions and guidelines:

- The name can be a maximum of 255 characters.

- The name must begin with either a letter or the underscore character (_). For the rest of the name, you can use any combination of characters, numbers, or symbols (except spaces). For multiple-word names, separate the words by using the underscore character or by mixing case (for example, Cost_Of_Goods or CostOfGoods). Excel doesn't distinguish between uppercase and lowercase letters in range names.

- Don't use cell addresses (such as Q1) or any of the operator symbols (such as +, −, *, /, <, >, and &), because these can cause confusion if you use the name in a formula.

- Range names that begin with R or C followed by one or more numbers are not allowed because of conflicts with the R1C1 reference style, where each cell is referenced by its row number followed by its column number (such as R1C1 or R8C2).

- To make typing easier, try to keep names as short as possible while still keeping them meaningful. TotalProfit2016 is faster to type than Total_Profit_For_Fiscal_Year_2016, and it's certainly clearer than the more cryptic TotPft16.

- Don't use any of the built-in names in Excel: Auto_Activate, Auto_Close, Auto_Deactivate, Auto_Open, Consolidate_Area, Criteria, Data_Form, Database, Extract, FilterDatabase, Print_Area, Print_Titles, Recorder, and Sheet_Title.

Name a cell or range

To name a cell or range, you can use either the Name box at the left end of the formula bar or the Define Name command.

The Name box usually shows the address of the active cell. However, after you define a name for a cell or range, it appears in the Name box whenever you select the cell or range. The Name box doubles as a drop-down list. To select a named range quickly, expand the list and select the name you want. Excel moves to the range and selects the cells.

Tip The Name box is resizable, so if you can't see all of the current name, point to the right edge of the Name box and drag the edge to resize the box.

You can also use the Name box to define a new name by selecting the cell or range and then entering the name directly into the Name box.

Click the Name box list to see the other defined names in the workbook

For a bit more control over the naming process, you can use the New Name dialog box. In this dialog box, you can not only specify the name and the range coordinates, you can also add a comment about the name and specify the scope of the name. The *scope* tells you the extent to which the range name will be recognized in formulas. You have two choices:

- **Workbook scope** This means the range name is available to all the sheets in a workbook (and is called a *workbook-level* name). This is the default scope, which means it's the scope that Excel assigns to any name you create by using the formula bar's Name box.

- **Worksheet scope** This means the range name is available only to a specified worksheet (and thus is called a *sheet-level* name). The name will refer only to the range on the sheet in which it was defined.

Use the New Name dialog box to gain more control over the naming process

To name a cell or range by using the Name box

1. Select the cell or range you want to name.

2. Click inside the **Name** box to display the insertion point.

3. Enter the name you want to use, and then press **Enter**. Excel defines the new name automatically.

To name a cell or range by using the New Name dialog box

1. Select the cell or range you want to name.

2. On the **Formulas** tab, in the **Defined Names** group, click **Define Name** to open the New Name dialog box.

3. Enter the range name in the **Name** text box.

4. Use the **Scope** list to select where you want the name to be available.

5. Use the **Comment** box to enter a description or other notes about the range name.

6. Click **OK** to define the name.

Name a table

When you create a table, Excel gives it the name *Table*n, where *n* means that this is the *n*th table added to the current workbook. Earlier in this book you learned how to reference table elements directly. Most of the time, these references include the table name, so you should consider giving your tables meaningful and unique names. For table names, follow the same rules and guidelines that were given for range names in the previous section.

To rename the active table

→ On the **Design** tool tab, in the **Properties** group, enter the table name in the **Table Name** box, and then press **Enter**.

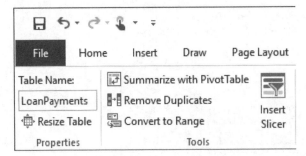

Name or rename a table on the Design tool tab

> **See Also** For information about how to reference table elements in a formula, see the topic "Reference table data by using structured references " topic in "Objective 1.1: Manage workbooks."

Manage named ranges and objects

Excel comes with a Name Manager feature, which is a useful interface for working with range or object names. You can use the Name Manager to change a name, edit a range name's coordinates, or to delete a name.

Name Manager				? ✕
New...	**Edit...**	**Delete**		**Filter ▾**
Name	**Value**	**Refers To**		**Scope**
▭ Amount	10,000	=Amortization!$B$6		Workbook
▭ Rate	5%	=Amortization!$B$4		Workbook
▭ Term	3	=Amortization!$B$5		Workbook

Refers to:
=Amortization!$B$6

Close

Edit and delete range and object names in the Name Manager

To edit a range or object name

1. On the **Formulas** tab, in the **Defined Names** group, click **Name Manager**.

2. In the **Name Manager** dialog box, click the name you want to edit.

3. Click **Edit** to open the Edit Name dialog box.

4. Make your changes to the name, and then click **OK**.

5. Click **Close** to close the Name Manager dialog box.

To delete a range or object name

1. In the **Name Manager** dialog box, click the name you want to delete.

2. Click **Delete**. Excel asks you to confirm the deletion.

3. Click **OK**, and then click **Close** to close the Name Manager dialog box.

Objective 3.6 practice tasks

The practice file for these tasks is located in the **MOSExcelExpert2016
\Objective3** practice file folder. The folder also contains a result file that
you can use to check your work.

➤ Open the **ExcelExpert_3-6** workbook, display the **Amortization**
worksheet, and do the following:

❑ Define the names <u>C_Rate</u> for cell B4, <u>C_Term</u> for cell B5, and <u>C_
Amount</u> for cell B6.

❑ Edit the formulas in cells E4:G30 to reference the cell names.

❑ Change the name defined for cell B4 to <u>Rate</u>, for cell B5 to <u>Term</u>, and
for cell B6 to <u>Amount</u>.

❑ Change the defined name of the table on the **Parts** worksheet to
<u>Parts</u>.

➤ Save the workbook.

➤ Open the **ExcelExpert_3-6_results** workbook. Compare the two
workbooks to check your work, and then close the open workbooks.

Objective group 4

Create advanced charts and tables

The skills tested in this section of the Microsoft Office Specialist Expert exam for Microsoft Excel 2016 relate to creating charts, PivotTables, and PivotCharts. Specifically, the following objectives are associated with this set of skills:

- **4.1** Create advanced charts
- **4.2** Create and manage PivotTables
- **4.3** Create and manage PivotCharts

Worksheets and external databases can contain hundreds of thousands or even millions of records. Analyzing that much data can be extremely difficult without the right kinds of tools. To help you, Excel offers three powerful data analysis tools: charts, PivotTables, and PivotCharts. By using these tools, you can visualize or summarize a large dataset in a concise format.

This chapter guides you in studying advanced charting techniques, including adding trendlines, creating charts with second value axes, and working with chart templates. You also learn how to create and modify PivotTables and how to use them to analyze data. Finally, you learn how to create PivotCharts that you can use to visualize and analyze your data at the same time.

4

> To complete the practice tasks in this chapter, you need the practice files contained in the **MOSExcelExpert2016\Objective4** practice file folder. For more information, see "Download the practice files" in this book's introduction.

Objective 4.1: Create advanced charts

This topic shows you several methods for creating advanced charts, including how to add various types of trendlines to a chart, how to configure a chart with a second value axis, and how to save a chart's layout and formatting as a template.

Tip The information in this book assumes that you know basic Excel chart techniques, including how to create a chart, how to work with chart types, and how to select and format chart elements. If you need a refresher, see *MOS 2016 Study Guide for Microsoft Excel* by Joan Lambert (Microsoft Press, 2017).

Add trendlines to charts

Regression analysis is a powerful statistical procedure that has become a popular business tool. In its general form, you use regression analysis to determine the relationship between two phenomena, one of which depends on the other. For example, car sales might be dependent on interest rates, and units sold might be dependent on the amount spent on advertising. The dependent phenomenon is called the *dependent variable*, or the y-value, and the phenomenon upon which it's dependent is called the *independent variable*, or the x-value. (Think of a chart on which the independent variable is plotted along the horizontal [x] axis and the dependent variable is plotted along the vertical [y] axis.)

Given these variables, you can do two things with regression analysis:

- Determine the relationship between the known x-values and y-values and use the results to calculate and visualize the overall trend of the data.
- Use the existing trend to forecast new y-values.

This objective covers *simple regression analysis*, which you use when you're dealing with only one independent variable. For example, if the dependent variable is car sales, the independent variable might be interest rates. How you analyze your data depends on whether it's linear or nonlinear. If data is *linear*, when you plot it on a chart, the resulting data points resemble (roughly) a straight line. If data is *nonlinear*, the resulting data points on a chart form a curve.

You can analyze both linear and nonlinear models by examining the trend underlying the current data you have for the dependent variable. One way to analyze the current trend is by calculating the *line of best fit*, or the *trendline*. This is a line through the data points for which the differences between the points above and below the line cancel each other out (more or less). If the independent variable is time, you can also use the trendline to create a forecast for the dependent variable.

Tip Not all Excel chart types support trendlines. You can add trendlines to two-dimensional area, bar, column, line, stock, XY (scatter), and bubble charts that aren't of a stacked type.

On an Excel chart, you can add six types of trendlines:

- **Linear** You use this straight-line trendline when the dependent variable is related to the independent variable by some constant factor. For example, you might find that car sales (the dependent variable) increase by 1 million units whenever interest rates (the independent variable) decrease by 1 percent. Similarly, you might find that division revenue (the dependent variable) increases by $100,000 for every $10,000 you spend on advertising (the independent variable).

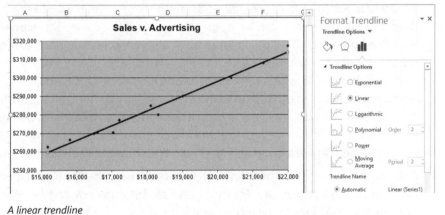

A linear trendline

- **Exponential** An *exponential* trend is one that rises or falls at an increasingly higher rate. Fads often exhibit this kind of behavior. This is called an exponential trend because its trendline looks much like a number being raised to successively higher values of an exponent (for example, 101, 102, 103, and so on).

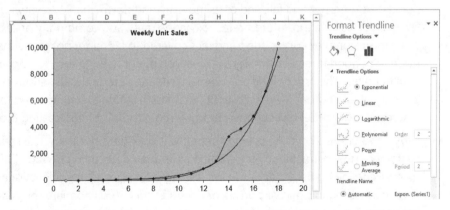

An exponential trendline

- **Logarithmic** A *logarithmic* trend is the inverse of an exponential trend: the values rise (or fall) quickly in the beginning and then level off. This is a common pattern in business. For example, a new company hires many people up front, and then hiring slows over time. A new product often sells many units soon after it's launched, and then sales level off. This pattern is described as logarithmic because it's typified by the shape of the curve made by a natural logarithm.

- **Power** A *power* trend is a pattern that curves steadily in one direction. The exponential and logarithmic trendlines are both "extreme" in the sense that they have radically different velocities at different parts of the curve. The exponential trendline begins slowly and then takes off at an ever-increasing pace; the logarithmic trendline begins quickly and then levels off. Most measurable business scenarios don't exhibit such extreme behavior. Revenues, profits, margins, and employee head count often tend to increase steadily over time (in successful companies, anyway). If you're analyzing a dependent variable that increases (or decreases) steadily with respect to some independent variable, but the linear trendline doesn't give a good fit, you should try a power trendline.

- **Polynomial** A *polynomial* trendline is a curve constructed out of an equation that uses multiple powers of *x*. For example, a *second-order* polynomial regression equation takes the following general form: $y = m_2 x^2 + m_1 x + b$ (where the values m_2, m_1, and b are constants). Use a polynomial trendline when the trend is not unidirectional, as in the linear, exponential, logarithmic, and power trends. Those trendlines are useful if the curve formed by the dependent variable values is also unidirectional, but that's often not the case in a business environment. Sales fluctuate, profits rise and fall, and costs move up and down, thanks to varying factors such as inflation, interest rates, exchange rates, and commodity prices. For these more complex curves, the trendlines covered so far might not give either a good fit or good forecasts. If that's the case, you might need to turn to a polynomial trendline. The *order* of the polynomial trendline determines its sensitivity. In general, a higher order gives a closer fit but is less accurate as a forecasting tool, whereas a lower order gives a looser fit but is more useful as a forecasting tool.

- **Moving Average** A *moving average* trendline is one that smooths a data series by averaging the series values over a specified number of preceding periods. This is a useful trendline for data that doesn't fit a straight line (linear), a unidirectional line (exponential, logarithmic, or power), or a regular curve (polynomial). The *period* of the moving is the number of periods used to calculate each average (that is, each point on the trendline). In general, a higher period gives a closer fit but is less accurate as a forecasting tool, whereas a lower period gives a looser fit but is more useful as a forecasting tool.

To add a trendline to a chart

1. Click the chart and, if more than one data series is plotted, click the series you want to work with.

2. On the **Design** tab, in the **Chart Layouts** group, click **Add Chart Element**, point to **Trendline**, and then do either of the following:

   - Click the type of trendline you want.
   - Click **More Trendline Options** to display the Trendline Options page of the Format Trendline pane, and then do the following:

     i. Select the type of trendline you want to add.

     ii. For a polynomial trendline, in the **Order** box, select the order of the polynomial equation you want; for a moving average trendline, in the **Period** box, select the period of the moving average calculation.

To forecast by using an existing trendline

1. Right-click the trendline to which you want to add forecasted values, and then click **Format Trendline** to display the Trendline Options page of the Format Trendline pane.

2. In the **Forecast** area, do either or both of the following:

   - In the **Forward** box, enter the number of units you want to project the trendline into the future. For example, to extend quarterly values into the next year, set Forward to 4 to extend the trendline by four quarters.
   - In the **Backward** box, enter the number of units you want to project the trendline into the past. For example, to extend monthly values into the previous year, set Backward to 12 to extend the trendline by 12 months.

Create dual-axis charts

If you show two or more data series in a single chart, you can change the chart type for one or more series and create a combination chart. By using different chart types, you can make it easier for your readers to distinguish different categories of data shown in the same chart. For example, you can create a combination chart that shows the number of homes sold as a line chart and the average sales price as a column chart.

However, when you plot two different types of data in the same chart, the range of values can vary wildly. For example, the values for homes sold might be measured in the tens of units, whereas the values for the average sales price might be measured in the hundreds of thousands. How can you combine these two disparate data sources so that you can see both series properly? The trick is to add another vertical axis—called the *secondary axis*—and have Excel plot one of the series by using that axis. This will

4

make it easier for the reader to see values for the associated series. In the example, you could plot average sales prices on one vertical axis and the number of homes sold on the other vertical axis.

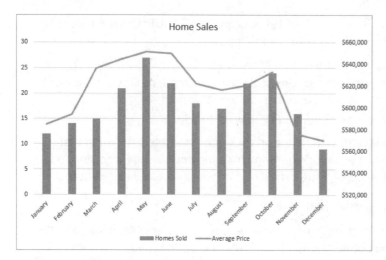

A dual-axis chart of home sales with units sold on the main vertical axis and average price on the secondary vertical axis

To change a selected chart to a dual-axis chart

1. On the **Design** tab, in the **Type** group, click **Change Chart Type** to open the Change Chart Type dialog box.

2. On the **All Charts** tab, in the category list, click **Combo**.

3. For each series, in the **Chart Type** list, select the chart type you want to apply.

4. For one of the series, select the **Secondary Axis** check box.

Choose the chart type and axis for your data series:

Series Name	Chart Type	Secondary Axis
Homes Sold	Clustered Column	☐
Average Price	Line	☑

Creating a dual-axis chart

5. Click **OK** to close the Change Chart Type dialog box and return to the worksheet.

Save a chart as a template

After you've changed a chart's type and performed other chart-related chores such as applying titles, adding labels, and choosing a layout, you might want to repeat the same settings for another chart. Rather than repeating the procedure to create the second chart, you can make your life easier by saving the original chart as a chart template and then creating the second chart (and any subsequent charts) based on this template. By default, chart templates are stored in the C:\Users*user name*\AppData\Roaming \Microsoft\Templates\Charts folder.

To save a chart as a template

1. Right-click the chart's plot area or background, and then click **Save as Template**.

2. Enter a name for the template, and then click **Save**.

To create a new chart based on a template

1. Select the range of data you want to chart.

2. On the **Insert** tab, in the **Charts** group, click **Recommended Charts**.

3. Click the **All Charts** tab, and then click **Templates**.

4. Click the template you want to use, and then click **OK**.

To apply a template to a selected chart

1. In the **Change Chart Type** dialog box, on the **All Charts** tab, click **Templates**.

2. Click the template you want to use, and then click **OK**.

4

Objective 4. 1 practice tasks

The practice file for these tasks is located in the **MOSExcelExpert2016 \Objective4** practice file folder. The folder also contains a result file that you can use to check your work.

➤ Open the **ExcelExpert_4-1** workbook and do the following:

- ❑ On the **Sales v. Advertising** worksheet, create a linear trendline for the displayed chart.

- ❑ On the **Employees** worksheet, add a logarithmic trendline to the existing chart.

- ❑ On the **Profits** worksheet, add a polynomial trendline with an order of **2** to the upper chart, and a polynomial trendline with an order of **6** to the lower chart.

- ❑ On the **Forecast** worksheet, create a linear trendline that extends into the future by four quarters.

- ❑ On the **Home Sales** worksheet, convert the existing chart to a dual-axis chart with the Average Price data series plotted on the secondary axis.

- ❑ Save the dual-axis Home Sales chart in the practice file folder as a chart template named <u>DualAxis</u>.

- ❑ Open the **Insert Chart** dialog box, click the **Templates** category, and confirm that it contains your chart template.

➤ Save the workbook.

➤ Open the **ExcelExpert_4-1_results** workbook. Compare the two workbooks to check your work. Then close the open workbooks.

Objective 4.2: Create and manage PivotTables

As mentioned at the beginning of this chapter, Excel comes with some powerful tools that can help you analyze the hundreds—or perhaps thousands—of records that can be contained in a table or external database. One of the most powerful of these data analysis tools is the PivotTable. You can use this tool to summarize hundreds of records in a concise tabular format. You can then manipulate the layout of the table to see different views of your data.

In the simplest case, PivotTables work by summarizing the data in one field (called a *data field*) and breaking it down according to the data in another field. The unique values in the second field (called the *row field*) become the row headings. For example, consider a workbook that has a table of sales by sales representatives that also includes columns for the region and quarter. With a PivotTable, you can summarize the numbers in the Sales field (the data field) and break them down by Region (the row field). In the resulting PivotTable (on a second worksheet), Excel uses the unique items in the Region field (for example, East, Midwest, South, and West) as row headings.

	B	C	D	E			A	B	C
	Region ▾	Quarter ▾	Sales Rep ▾	Sales ▾		1			
	East	1st	Steven Buchanan	$192,345		2			
	West	1st	Michael Suyama	$210,880		3		Region ▾	Sum of Sales
	East	1st	Margaret Peacock	$185,223		4		East	$1,463,655
	South	1st	Janet Leverling	$165,778		5		Midwest	$1,365,215
	Midwest	1st	Anne Dodsworth	$155,557		6		South	$1,409,544
	South	1st	Nancy Davolio	$180,567		7		West	$1,477,884
	West	1st	Laura Callahan	$200,767		8		Grand Total	$5,716,298
	Midwest	1st	Andrew Fuller	$165,663		9			
	East	2nd	Steven Buchanan	$173,493		10			
	West	2nd	Michael Suyama	$200,203		11			
	East	2nd	Margaret Peacock	$170,213		12			
	South	2nd	Janet Leverling	$155,339		13			
	Midwest	2nd	Anne Dodsworth	$148,990		14			
	South	2nd	Nancy Davolio	$175,660		15			
	West	2nd	Laura Callahan	$190,290		16			
	Midwest	2nd	Andrew Fuller	$159,002		17			
	East	3rd	Steven Buchanan	$175,776		18			

| Sales | Sales By Region | Quarterly Sales By Region | ⊕ | | | ◄ ► | Sales | **Sales By Region** | ... ⊕ |

4

A PivotTable summarizes the data from the original table by showing total sales broken down by region

Create PivotTables

PivotTables look complex to build, but creating a basic PivotTable takes just a few steps. You can also build fancier PivotTables; Excel offers a wide range of options, styles, and features.

The most common source for a PivotTable is an Excel table, although you can also use data that's set up as a regular range. You can use just about any table or range to build a PivotTable, but the best candidates for PivotTables exhibit two main characteristics:

- At least one of the fields contains *groupable* data. That is, the field contains data with a limited number of distinct text, numeric, or date values. In the Sales worksheet example, the Region field is perfect for a PivotTable because, despite having dozens of items, it has only four distinct values: East, West, Midwest, and South.

- Each field in the list must have a heading.

Excel can also put together a PivotTable even if your source data exists in an external database (for example, a Microsoft Access or SQL Server database). If you have existing data connections on your system, you can use one of them as the data source. Otherwise, you can create a new connection as needed.

Create a PivotTable by using options in the Create PivotTable dialog box

You build a PivotTable visually by using the PivotTable Fields pane, which displays the available fields and offers four regions to which you can add one or more fields:

- **Rows** In this area, you specify the PivotTable's *row field*, which displays vertically the unique values from the field.

- **Columns** In this area, you specify the PivotTable's *column field*, which displays horizontally the unique values from the field.

- **Values** In this area, you specify the PivotTable's *data field*, which displays the results of the calculation that Excel applies to the field's numeric data.

- **Filters** In this area, you specify the PivotTable's *filter field*, which displays a drop-down list that contains the unique values from the field. When you select a value from the list, Excel filters the PivotTable results to include only the records that match the selected value.

In the PivotTable Fields pane, you drag fields into some or all of the four areas: Rows, Columns, Values, and Filters

To create a PivotTable from an Excel table or range

1. Click inside the table or range.

2. On the **Insert** tab, in the **Tables** group, click **PivotTable** to open the Create PivotTable dialog box.

3. Click **Select a table or range**. The table name or the range address should already appear in the Table/Range box. If it does not, enter or select the table name or range address.

4. Below **Choose where you want the PivotTable report to be placed**, do either of the following:

    - Select **New Worksheet** (the default) to have Excel create a new worksheet for the PivotTable.

    - Select **Existing Worksheet** and then, in the **Location** box, enter or select the cell where you want to anchor the upper-left corner of the PivotTable.

5. Click **OK**. Excel displays the PivotTable Fields pane and two PivotTable Tools tabs: Analyze and Design.

6. Add fields to the PivotTable by doing either of the following:

    - In the **Choose fields to add to report** list, select the check box beside each field you want to add. Excel adds numeric fields to the Values area and text fields to the Rows area.

    - Drag each field and drop it inside the area where you want the field to appear.

    Tip If you're using an exceptionally large data source, it might take Excel a long time to update the PivotTable as you add each field. If this is the case, select the Defer Layout Update check box, which tells Excel not to update the PivotTable as you add each field. When you're ready to see the current PivotTable layout, click Update.

To create a PivotTable from an external data source

1. On the **Insert** tab, in the **Tables** group, click **PivotTable** to open the Create PivotTable dialog box.

2. Select **Use an external data source**, and then click **Choose Connection**.

3. If the connection you want to use is listed, click it and then click **Open**. Otherwise, do the following:

    a. Click **Browse for More** to open the Select Data Source dialog box.

    b. Click **New Source** to start the Data Connection Wizard.

    c. Click the type of data source you want, and then click **Next**.

    d. Specify the data source. (The method depends on the type of data source. For SQL Server, you specify the server name and sign-in credentials; for an ODBC data source, such as an Access database, you specify the database file.)

    e. Select the database and table you want to use, and then click **Next**.

    f. Click **Finish** to complete the Data Connection Wizard.

4. Below **Choose where you want the PivotTable report to be placed**, select **New Worksheet** or **Existing Worksheet**.

5. Click **OK** to close the dialog box and go to the PivotTable.

6. Add fields to the PivotTable as described in the procedure "To create a PivotTable from an Excel table or range" earlier in this topic.

Modify PivotTable field selections and options

A PivotTable is a powerful data analysis tool because it can take hundreds or even thousands of records and summarize them into a compact, comprehensible report. But its usefulness goes beyond simple consolidation: unlike most of the other data-analysis features in Excel, a PivotTable is not a static collection of worksheet cells. Instead, you can move the fields to different parts of the PivotTable; sort the row, column, or data field; and filter the data to show only the items you want to view.

You can move a PivotTable's fields from one area of the PivotTable to another. By doing so, you can view your data from different perspectives, which can greatly enhance the analysis of the data. Moving a field within a PivotTable is called *pivoting* the data.

The most common way to pivot the data is to move fields between the row and column areas. If your PivotTable contains just a single nondata field, moving the field between the row and column areas changes the orientation of the PivotTable between horizontal (column area) and vertical (row area). If your PivotTable contains fields in both the row and column areas, pivoting one of those fields to the other area creates multiple fields in that area. For example, pivoting a field from the column area to the row area creates two fields in the row area.

When you create a PivotTable, Excel sorts the data in ascending order based on the items in the row and column fields. For example, if the row area contains the Product field, the vertical sort order of the PivotTable is ascending according to the items in the Product field. You can change this default sort order to one that suits your needs. Excel gives you two choices: you can switch between ascending and descending, or you can sort based on a data field instead of a row or column field.

Clicking the arrow in a row or column field's header opens a menu of sort and filter options

Sorting the PivotTable based on the values in a data field is useful when you want to rank the results. For example, if your PivotTable shows the sum of sales for each product, an ascending or descending sort of the product name enables you to easily find a particular product. However, if you are more interested in finding which products sold the most (or the least), you need to sort the PivotTable on the data field.

Right-clicking a data field displays a menu from which you can sort the results

By default, each PivotTable displays a summary for all the records in your source data. This is usually what you want to see. However, there might be situations in which you need to focus more closely on some aspect of the data. You can focus on a specific item from one of the source data fields by taking advantage of the PivotTable's filter field.

For example, suppose you are dealing with a PivotTable that summarizes data from thousands of customer invoices over some period of time. A basic PivotTable might tell you the total amount sold for each product that you carry. That is interesting, but what if you want to see the total amount sold for each product in a specific country/region? If the Product field is in the PivotTable's row area, you can add the Country/Region field to the column area. However, there might be dozens of countries/regions, so that is not an efficient solution. Instead, you can add the Country/Region field to the PivotTable filter. You can then have Excel display the total sold for each product for the specific country/region that you are interested in.

Country/Region	Canada	.T

Search 🔎

- (All)
- Argentina
- Austria
- Belgium
- Brazil
- Canada
- Denmark
- Finland
- France
- Germany

☐ Select Multiple Items

OK   Cancel

Row Labels
Alice Mutton
Aniseed Syrup
Boston Crab Meat
Camembert Pierrot
Chai
Côte de Blaye
Filo Mix
Fløtemysost
Geitost
Gnocchi di nonna Alice
Grandma's Boysenberr

Clicking the arrow in the filter field header displays possible filter values

You can also filter a PivotTable by using a row or column field. In this case, Excel filters the PivotTable data to show only the row or column items that you add to the filter.

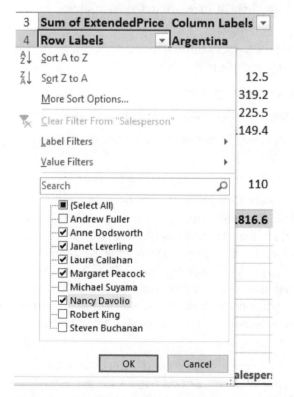

3	Sum of ExtendedPrice	Column Labels ▼
4	Row Labels ▼	Argentina

A↓ Sort A to Z
Z↓ Sort Z to A   12.5
More Sort Options...   319.2
                                        225.5
🍋 Clear Filter From "Salesperson"   149.4
Label Filters   ▶
Value Filters   ▶
Search 🔎   110
☑ (Select All)
☐ Andrew Fuller   .816.6
☑ Anne Dodsworth
☑ Janet Leverling
☑ Laura Callahan
☑ Margaret Peacock
☐ Michael Suyama
☑ Nancy Davolio
☐ Robert King
☐ Steven Buchanan

OK   Cancel
                                        alesper:

Clicking the arrow in the row or column field header displays possible filter values

4

To move a field to a different area

→ In the **PivotTable Fields** pane, drag the field you want to move from its current area to the new area.

To sort a PivotTable by using a row or column field

1. In the field header for the row or column field you want to use for sorting, click the arrow.
2. Click the sort order you want to use, such as **Sort Z to A**.

To sort a PivotTable by using a data field

1. Right-click any cell in the data field.
2. In the menu, point to **Sort**, and then click the sort order you want to use, such as **Sort Largest to Smallest**.

To filter PivotTable data by using the filter field

1. In the field header for the PivotTable's filter field, click the arrow.
2. Do either of the following, and then click **OK** to return to the PivotTable:
   - Click the item you want to use as the filter.
   - To apply multiple filters, select the **Select Multiple Items** check box, and then click each item you want to include in the filter.

To filter PivotTable data by using a row or column field

1. In the field header for the PivotTable's row or column field, click the arrow.
2. Clear the check box beside each item you do not want to view, and then click **OK**.

Create slicers

So far in this chapter, you have learned how to filter a PivotTable either by using the filter field, which applies to the entire PivotTable, or by using row or column items, which apply only to that field. In both cases, the filter is usable only with the PivotTable in which it is defined. However, it is not unusual to require the same filter in multiple PivotTables. For example, if you are a sales manager responsible for sales in a particular set of countries/regions, you might often need to filter a PivotTable to show data from just those countries/regions. Similarly, if you work with a subset of your company's product line, you might often have to filter PivotTables to show the results from just those products.

Applying these kinds of filters to one or two PivotTables is not difficult or time consuming, but if you have to apply the same filter over and over again, the process becomes frustrating and inefficient. To combat this, Excel offers a PivotTable feature called the *slicer*. A slicer is very similar to a filter field, except that it is independent of any PivotTable. This means that you can apply the same slicer to multiple PivotTables.

Row Labels	Sum of ExtendedPrice
Andrew Fuller	$57.50
Anne Dodsworth	$966.80
Janet Leverling	$8,922.35
Laura Callahan	$1,278.40
Margaret Peacock	$2,993.25
Michael Suyama	$1,078.00
Nancy Davolio	$6,807.19
Robert King	$9,194.56
Grand Total	**$31,298.05**

Country/Region

- Argentina
- Austria
- Belgium
- Brazil
- Canada
- Denmark
- Finland
- France

A slicer that applies a filter to any PivotTable that includes a Country/Region field

If your PivotTable includes one or more fields with dates, you can also create a *timeline slicer*, which displays a sliding timeline that you can use to select specific days, months, or years. Excel then filters the PivotTable to show the data only for the selected time value.

Row Labels	Sum of ExtendedPrice
Boston Crab Meat	$1,104.00
Camembert Pierrot	$1,020.00
Carnarvon Tigers	$5,100.00
Chai	$652.50
Chang	$1,871.50
Chartreuse verte	$643.50
Chef Anton's Cajun Seasoning	$748.00
Chef Anton's Gumbo Mix	$288.22
Escargots de Bourgogne	$79.50

OrderDate

Aug 2016   MONTHS

2016

JUN   JUL   AUG   SEP   OCT   NOV   DE

An example of a timeline slicer

To create and apply a slicer

1. Click a cell in a PivotTable that contains the field for which you want to create a slicer.

2. On the **Analyze** tab, in the **Filter** group, click **Insert Slicer** to open the Insert Slicers dialog box.

3. Select the check box beside each field for which you want to create the slicer, and then click **OK**. Excel displays one slicer for each field you selected.

4. In the slicer, click a field item that you want to include in your filter. If you want to include multiple items in your filter, hold down **Ctrl** while you click each item. Excel filters the PivotTable based on the field items you select in each slicer.

To create and apply a timeline slicer

1. Click a cell in a PivotTable that contains the field for which you want to create a slicer.

2. On the **Analyze** tab, in the **Filter** group, click **Insert Timeline** to open the Insert Timelines dialog box.

3. Select the check box beside each field for which you want to create a timeline slicer, and then click **OK**. Excel displays one timeline for each field you selected.

4. In the timeline's list, select a time unit: **Years**, **Quarters**, **Months**, or **Days**.

5. Click the time period you want to view. Excel filters the PivotTable based on the time period you select in each timeline.

Group PivotTable data

Most PivotTables have just a few items in the row and column fields, which makes the PivotTable easy to read and analyze. However, it is not unusual to have row or column fields that consist of dozens of items, which makes the PivotTable much more unwieldy. To make a PivotTable with a large number of row or column items easier to work with, you can group the items together. For example, you could group months into quarters, thus reducing the number of items from 12 to 4. Similarly, a PivotTable that lists dozens of countries/regions could group those countries/regions by continent, thus reducing the number of items to four or five, depending on where the countries/regions are located. Finally, if you use a numeric field in the row or column area, you might have hundreds of items, one for each numeric value. You can improve the PivotTable by creating just a few numeric ranges. In Excel, you can group three types of data: numeric, date and time, and text.

Grouping numeric values is useful when you use a numeric source for a row or column field. In Excel, you can specify numeric ranges into which the field items are grouped. For example, suppose you have a PivotTable of invoice data that shows the extended price (the row field) and the salesperson (the column field). It would be useful to group the extended prices into ranges and then count the number of invoices each salesperson processed in each range.

IMPORTANT The ranges that Excel creates after you apply the grouping to a numeric field are not themselves numeric values; they are, instead, text values. Unfortunately, this means it is not possible to use the AutoSort feature in Excel to switch the ranges from ascending order to descending order, because Excel sorts the items as text, not as numbers.

Count of ExtendedPrice	Column Labels ▾			
Row Labels ▾	Andrew Fuller	Anne Dodsworth	Janet Leverling	Laura Callahan
0-1000	83	38	156	109
1000-2000	10	4	19	13
2000-3000	7	1	6	2
3000-4000		2	1	
4000-5000	1			
5000-6000	1			
6000-7000			1	
7000-8000			1	
8000-9000				
10000-11000				
Grand Total	102	45	184	124

A PivotTable grouped in ranges of 1,000 according to the numeric values in the row field.

If your PivotTable includes a field with date or time data, you can use the grouping feature in Excel to consolidate that data into more manageable or useful groups. For example, a PivotTable based on a list of invoice data might show the total dollar amount, which is the Sum Of Extended Price in the data area, of the orders placed on each day, which is the Date field in the row area. Tracking daily sales is useful, but a manager might need a PivotTable that shows the bigger picture. In that case, you can use the Grouping feature to consolidate the dates into weeks, months, or even quarters. You can even choose multiple date groupings. For example, if you have several years' worth of invoice data, you could group the data into years, the years into quarters, and the quarters into months.

Row Labels ▾	Sum of ExtendedPrice
⊟ Qtr1	
Jan	$61,258.06
Feb	$38,483.63
Mar	$38,547.21
⊟ Qtr2	
Apr	$53,032.95
May	$53,781.28
Jun	$36,362.79
⊟ Qtr3	
Jul	$51,020.83
Aug	$47,287.66
Sep	$55,629.24
⊟ Qtr4	
Oct	$66,749.23
Nov	$43,533.79
Dec	$71,398.41
Grand Total	$617,085.08

A PivotTable grouped by quarters, and then by months, according to the date values in the row field

You can also group time data. For example, suppose you have data that shows the time of day that an assembly line completes each operation. If you want to analyze how the time of day affects productivity, you could set up a PivotTable that groups the data into minutes—for example, 30-minute intervals—or hours.

Finally, you can use the PivotTable Grouping feature to create custom groups from the text items in a row or column field. One common problem that arises when you work with PivotTables is that you often need to consolidate items, but you have no corresponding field in the data. For example, the data might have a Country/Region field, but what if you need to consolidate the PivotTable results by continent? It is unlikely that your source data includes a Continent field. Similarly, your source data might include employee names, but you might need to consolidate the employees according to the people they report to. What do you do if your source data does not include a Supervisor field?

The solution in both cases is to use the Grouping feature to create custom groups. For the country/region data, you could create custom groups named North America, South America, Europe, and so on. For the employees, you could create a custom group for each supervisor. You select the items that you want to include in a particular group, create the custom group, and then change the new group name to reflect its content.

Sum of ExtendedPrice	Column Labels			
Row Labels	Andrew Fuller	Anne Dodsworth	Janet Leverling	Laura Callahan
⊟South America				
Argentina		12.5	319.2	225.5
Brazil	5524.4		3389.64	4983.6
Venezuela	1600.5	378	5866.84	4109.98
⊟Europe				
Austria	6129.45	344	14595.45	5422.09
Denmark	1405.2		1684.27	48.75
Finland	5292.03	1590.56		4131.8
France	5279.51	1761	8907.52	3062.57
Germany	25984.1	7800.6	22430.68	11220.47
Ireland	2381.05	7403.9	2674.85	
Italy	3265.55	23.8	88	2078.86

A PivotTable grouped by continent according to the country/region names in the row field.

To group numeric data in a PivotTable

1. Click any item in the numeric field you want to group.

2. On the **Analyze** tab, in the **Group** section, click **Group Field** to open the Grouping dialog box.

3. Enter the starting and ending numeric values by doing one of the following:

    -   In the **Starting at** box, enter the starting numeric value, and in the **Ending at** box, enter the ending numeric value.

    -   Select either or both of the **Starting at** and **Ending at** check boxes to have Excel extract the minimum value and the maximum value, respectively, of the numeric items, and to place that value in the corresponding box.

4. In the **By** text box, enter the size you want to use for each grouping, and then click **OK** to return to the PivotTable.

In this version of the Grouping dialog box, you can set up your numeric groupings

To group date and time data in a PivotTable

1. Click any item in the date or time field you want to group, and open the **Grouping** dialog box.

2. Enter the starting and ending date or time values by doing one of the following:

    -   In the **Starting at** box, enter the starting date or time value, and in the **Ending at** box, enter the ending date or time value.

    -   Select either or both of the **Starting at** and **Ending at** check boxes to have Excel extract the minimum value and the maximum value, respectively, of the date or time items, and to place that value in the corresponding box.

3. In the **By** list, click the type of grouping you want. To use multiple groupings, click each type of grouping you want to use.

4. If you clicked only **Days** in step 3, in the **Number of days** box, specify the number of days to use as the group interval.

In this version of the Grouping dialog box, you can set up your date or time groupings.

5. Click **OK** to return to the PivotTable.

To group text data in a PivotTable

1. Select the items that you want to include in the group.

2. On the **Analyze** tab, in the **Group** section, click **Group Selection**. Excel creates a new group named Group*n* (where *n* means this is the *n*th group you have created) and restructures the PivotTable.

3. Click the group label, enter a new name for the group, and then press **Enter**. Excel renames the group.

4. Repeat steps 1 through 3 for the other items in the field until you have created all the groups you want.

Reference data in a PivotTable by using the GETPIVOTDATA function

What do you do when you need to include a PivotTable result in a regular worksheet formula? At first, you might be tempted just to include a reference to the appropriate cell in the PivotTable's data area. However, that works only if your PivotTable is static and never changes. In the vast majority of cases, the reference won't remain accurate because the addresses of the PivotTable values change as you pivot, filter, group, and refresh the PivotTable.

If you want to include a PivotTable result in a formula and you want that result to remain accurate even as you manipulate the PivotTable, use the GETPIVOTDATA function. This function uses the data field, PivotTable location, and one or more (row or column) field/item pairs that specify the exact value to use. Here's the syntax:

GETPIVOTDATA(data_field, pivot_table[, field1, item1...])

The following table describes the GETPIVOTDATA function arguments.

Argument	Description
data_field	The name of the PivotTable data field that contains the data you want
pivot_table	The address of any cell or range within the PivotTable, or a named range within the PivotTable
field1	The name of the PivotTable row or column field that contains the data you want
item1	The name of the item within *field1* that specifies the data you want

Note that you always enter the *field*n and *item*n arguments as a pair. If you don't include any field/item pairs, GETPIVOTDATA returns the PivotTable grand total. You can enter up to 126 field/item pairs. This might make GETPIVOTDATA seem like more work than it's worth, but the good news is that you'll rarely have to enter the GETPIVOTDATA function manually. By default, Excel is configured to generate the appropriate GETPIVOTDATA syntax automatically. That is, you start your worksheet formula, and when you get to the part where you need the PivotTable value, just click the value. Excel then inserts the GETPIVOTDATA function by using the syntax that returns the value you want.

F5	:	×	✓	*fx*	=GETPIVOTDATA("Extended Price",$A$3,"Country/Region","Argentina","Shipper","Federal Shipping")

⊿	A	B	C	D	E	F
2						
3	Sum of Extended Price	Column Labels ▾				
4	Row Labels ▾	Federal Shipping	Speedy Express	United Package	Grand Total	
5	Argentina	$1,197.80	$1,387.00	$3,717.70	$6,302.50	$1,197.80
6	Austria	$22,284.83	$23,089.38	$25,227.78	$70,601.99	
7	Belgium	$5,327.00	$295.38	$16,767.99	$22,390.37	

A formula that uses GETPIVOTDATA to reference a value in a PivotTable

To reference PivotTable data by using the GETPIVOTDATA function

➔ Enter your formula up to the point where you want to insert the GETPIVOTDATA function, and then click the PivotTable data field value you want to use.

Add calculated fields

By default, Excel uses a Sum function for calculating the data field summaries. Although Sum is the most common summary function used in PivotTables, it's not the only one. Excel offers the 11 summary functions outlined in the following table.

Function	Description
Sum	Adds the values for the underlying data
Count	Displays the total number of values in the underlying data
Average	Calculates the average of the values for the underlying data
Max	Returns the largest value for the underlying data
Min	Returns the smallest value for the underlying data
Product	Calculates the product of the values for the underlying data
Count Numbers	Displays the total number of numeric values in the underlying data
StdDev	Calculates the standard deviation of the values for the underlying data, treated as a sample
StdDevp	Calculates the standard deviation of the values for the underlying data, treated as a population
Var	Calculates the variance of the values for the underlying data, treated as a sample
Varp	Calculates the variance of the values for the underlying data, treated as a population

You can use summary functions to create powerful and useful PivotTables, but they don't cover every data analysis possibility. For example, suppose you have a PivotTable that uses the Sum function to summarize invoice totals by sales representative. That's useful, but you might also want to pay out a bonus to those representatives whose total sales exceed some threshold. You could use the GETPIVOTDATA function to create regular worksheet formulas to calculate whether bonuses should be paid and how much they should be (assuming each bonus is a percentage of the total sales).

However, this isn't very convenient. If you add sales representatives, you need to add formulas; if you remove sales representatives, existing formulas generate errors. And, in any case, one of the points of generating a PivotTable is to perform fewer worksheet calculations, not more. The solution in this case is to take advantage of the *calculated field* feature. A calculated field is a new data field based on a custom formula.

For example, if your invoice's PivotTable has an Extended Price field and you want to award a 5-percent bonus to those representatives who did at least $75,000 worth of business, you'd create a calculated field based on the following formula:

=IF('Extended Price' >= 75000, 'Extended Price' * 0.05, 0)

IMPORTANT When you reference a field in your formula, Excel interprets this reference as the sum of that field's values. For example, if you include the logical expression 'Extended Price' >= 75000 in a calculated field formula, Excel interprets this as "Sum of 'Extended Price' >= 75000." That is, it adds the values in the Extended Price field together and then compares the result with 75000.

A slightly different PivotTable problem is when a field you're using for the row or column labels doesn't contain an item you need. For example, suppose your products are organized into various categories, such as Beverages, Condiments, Confections, and Dairy Products. Suppose further that these categories are grouped into several divisions—for example, Beverages and Condiments in Division A, and Confections and Dairy Products in Division B. If the source data doesn't have a Division field, how do you see PivotTable results that apply to the divisions?

One solution is to create groups for each division, as described earlier in this objective. That works, but Excel gives you a second solution: use calculated items. A *calculated item* is a new item in a row or column where the item's values are generated by a custom formula. For example, you could create a new item named *Division A* that is based on the following formula:

=Beverages + Condiments

To change the data field summary calculation

1. Do either of the following:
   - Right-click any cell inside the data field, and then point to **Summarize Values By** to display a partial list of the available summary calculations. If you see the calculation you want, click it; otherwise, click **More Options** to open the Value Field Settings dialog box.
   - Click any cell in the data field. Then on the **Analyze** tab, in the **Active Field** group, click **Field Settings** to open the Value Field Settings dialog box.
2. In the **Summarize value field by** list, click the summary calculation you want to use. Then click **OK** to return to the worksheet.

To add a calculated field

1. Click any cell inside the data field.

2. On the **Analyze** tab, in the **Calculations** group, click **Fields, Items, & Sets** and then click **Calculated Field** to open the Insert Calculated Field dialog box.

3. In the **Name** box, enter a name for the calculated field.

4. In the **Formula** box, enter the formula you want to use for the calculated field.

    > **Tip** If you need to use a field name in the formula, position the cursor where you want the field name to appear, click the field name in the Fields list, and then click Insert Field.

5. Click **Add**, and then click **OK**.

To add a calculated item

1. Click any cell inside the row or column field to which you want to add the item.

2. On the **Analyze** tab, in the **Calculations** group, click **Fields, Items, & Sets** and then click **Calculated Item** to open the Insert Calculated Item In "*Field*" dialog box (where *Field* is the name of the field you're working with).

3. In the **Name** box, enter a name for the calculated item.

4. In the **Formula** box, enter the formula you want to use for the calculated item.

5. Click **Add**, and then click **OK**.

Format data

When you click any cell within a PivotTable, Excel displays the PivotTable Tools tool tabs, one of which is named *Design*. You can use the controls on the Design tool tab to perform six different PivotTable formatting tasks:

- **Configure subtotals** If you group your PivotTable values, you can configure the group subtotals to appear either at the bottom or the top of the group, or you can turn off the subtotals altogether.

- **Configure grand totals** You can set the PivotTable grand totals to appear for both rows and columns, for rows only, for columns only, or not at all.

- **Select a report layout** If you display more than one field in an area of the PivotTable, you can change the order of those fields if you want a different view of your report. When you have multiple fields in the row area, Excel displays each field in its own column, the field and subfield items all begin on the same row, and gridlines appear around every cell. This is called the *tabular layout* and is the default PivotTable layout. Excel also comes with two other report layouts that you can use. The *outline layout* also displays each field in its own column. However, the subfield items for each field item begin one row below the field item, and no gridlines appear around the cells (except for a single gridline under each item in the outer field). The *compact layout* displays each field in a single column. The subfield items for each field item begin one row below the field item and are indented from the left. No gridlines appear around the cells (except for a single gridline under each item in the outer field).

- **Add or remove blank rows** If you have multiple fields in the row or column area, you can elect to add a blank row between each item, which can often make the PivotTable easier to read.

- **Set PivotTable style options** You can turn on or off the PivotTable row headers, column headers, banded rows, and banded columns.

- **Apply a PivotTable style** A style is a collection of formatting options—fonts, borders, and background colors—that Excel defines for different areas of a PivotTable. For example, a style might use bold, white text on a black background for labels and grand totals, and white text on a dark blue background for items and data.

To format PivotTable data

1. Click any cell inside the PivotTable.

2. On the **Design** tab, in the **Layout** group, do any of the following:
   - Click **Subtotals**, and then click one of the options in the list.
   - Click **Grand Totals**, and then click one of the options in the list.
   - Click **Report Layout**, and then click one of the options in the list.
   - Click **Blank Rows**, and then click one of the options to add or remove blank rows.

3. In the **PivotTable Style Options** group, select or clear the check boxes to turn the **Row Headers**, **Column Headers**, **Banded Rows**, and **Banded Columns** features on or off.

4. In the **PivotTable Styles** group, in the gallery, click a predefined style to apply it to the PivotTable.

4

Objective 4.2 practice tasks

The practice file for these tasks is located in the **MOSExcelExpert2016 \Objective4** practice file folder. The folder also contains a result file that you can use to check your work.

➤ Open the **ExcelExpert_4-2** workbook.

➤ From the table on the **Invoices** worksheet, create a PivotTable, place it on a new worksheet, and do the following:

   ❑ Rename the worksheet <u>By Salesperson</u>.

   ❑ In the PivotTable, summarize the values in the ExtendedPrice field by Salesperson.

   ❑ Add a calculated field named <u>Bonus</u> that calculates a 5-percent bonus for the salespeople with sales of at least $75,000 and 0 for salespeople who sold less than that amount. (The field name will change after you create it to *Sum of Bonus*.)

➤ From the table on the **Invoices** worksheet, create a PivotTable, place it on a new worksheet, and do the following:

   ❑ Rename the worksheet <u>By Category</u>.

   ❑ In the PivotTable, summarize the values in the Quantity field by both the Country/Region field (as the row field) and the Category field (as the column field).

   ❑ Switch the row and column fields.

   ❑ Create a timeline slicer based on the OrderDate field.

➤ From the table on the **Invoices** worksheet, create a PivotTable, place it on a new worksheet, and do the following:

   ❑ Rename the worksheet <u>By Price</u>.

   ❑ In the PivotTable, summarize the Quantity field by UnitPrice.

   ❑ Group the UnitPrice field in $10 increments from $0 to $270.

   ❑ In cell A1, enter <u>Units sold in the lowest price range:</u> in bold, and then, in cell D1, create a formula that returns the number of units sold in the *0-10* group.

➤ Save the **ExcelExpert_4-2** workbook. Open the **ExcelExpert_4-2_results** workbook. Compare the two workbooks to check your work. Then close the open workbooks.

Objective 4.3: Create and manage PivotCharts

A PivotChart is a graphical representation of the values in a PivotTable. However, a PivotChart goes far beyond a regular chart, because a PivotChart has many of the same capabilities as a PivotTable. These capabilities include hiding items, filtering data by using the filter field, and refreshing the PivotChart to account for changes in the underlying data. Also, if you move fields from one area of the PivotTable to another, the PivotChart changes accordingly. You also have access to most of the regular charting capabilities in Excel, so PivotCharts are a powerful addition to your data-analysis toolkit.

Create PivotCharts

Excel offers three ways to create a PivotChart:

- You can create a PivotChart directly from an existing PivotTable. This saves time because you do not have to configure the layout of the PivotChart or any other options. When you use this method, Excel uses the default chart type for the data and places the PivotChart on a new chart sheet.

- You can create a PivotChart on the same worksheet as its associated PivotTable. That way you can easily compare the PivotTable and the PivotChart. This is called *embedding* the PivotChart on the worksheet.

- If the data you want to summarize and visualize exists as an Excel table or range, you can build a PivotChart directly from that data. Note, however, that Excel does not allow you to create just a PivotChart on its own. Instead, Excel creates a PivotTable and an embedded PivotChart at the same time. If you want to analyze your data by using both a PivotTable and a PivotChart, this method will save you time because it does not require any extra steps to embed the PivotChart along with the PivotTable.

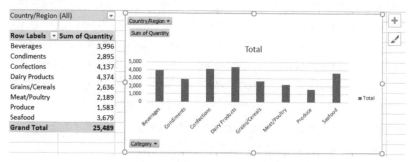

A PivotChart embedded on the same worksheet as its PivotTable

To create a PivotChart of the default type on a new sheet from a PivotTable

→ Click any cell in the PivotTable, and then press **F11**.

To embed a PivotChart on the same worksheet as a PivotTable

1. Click any cell in the PivotTable.

2. Do either of the following to open the Insert Chart dialog box:

   - On the **Analyze** tab, in the **Tools** group, click **PivotChart**.
   - On the **Insert** tab, in the **Charts** group, click the **PivotChart** button (not the arrow).

3. In the category list, click the chart type you want.

   > **IMPORTANT** You can't use charts in the XY (Scatter), Stock, Treemap, Sunburst, Histogram, Box And Whisker, Waterfall, or Funnel categories to create a PivotChart from a PivotTable.

4. On the chart category page, click the chart subtype you want. Then click **OK** to close the dialog box and return to the worksheet.

To create a PivotChart from an Excel table or range

1. Click inside the table or range.

2. On the **Insert** tab, in the **Charts** group, click **PivotChart** to open the Create PivotChart dialog box.

3. Click **Select a table or range**. The table name or the range address should already appear in the **Table/Range** box. If it does not, enter or select the table name or range address.

4. Do either of the following:

   - Select **New Worksheet** (the default) to have Excel create a new worksheet for the PivotChart.
   - Select **Existing Worksheet** and then, in the **Location** box, enter or select the cell where you want to anchor the upper-left corner of the PivotChart.

5. Click **OK**. Excel creates the PivotTable and PivotChart skeletons and displays the PivotTable Fields pane and three PivotChart Tools tabs: Analyze, Design, and Format.

6. Add the fields you want to the PivotTable. As you add each field, Excel updates both the PivotTable and the PivotChart.

Modify PivotCharts

By default, each PivotChart displays a summary for all the records in your source data. This is usually what you want to see. However, there might be situations where you need to focus more closely on some aspect of the data. You can do this by changing the PivotChart's row, column, and filter options:

- Click the row field button in the lower-left corner to sort the row items, apply a filter to the row items, or hide one or more row items.

- Click the column field button just above the chart legend to sort the column items, apply a filter to the column items, or hide one or more column items.

- Click the filter field button in the upper-left corner to apply one or more filters to the entire PivotChart.

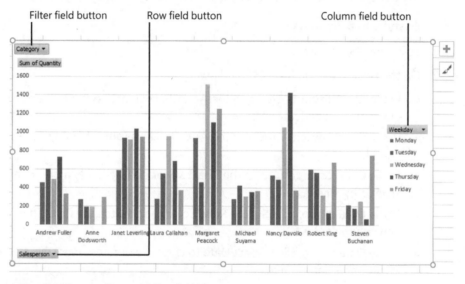

A PivotChart's row, column, and filter field buttons

When you select a PivotChart, the PivotChart tool tabs appear. The Design tool tab includes several options for changing the PivotChart style:

- **Adding chart elements** You can modify the chart by adding elements such as a chart title, axis titles, data labels, a data table, and gridlines.

- **Applying a predefined chart layout** Excel offers 11 preset chart layouts that you can use to quickly display titles, gridlines, and other chart elements.

- **Changing the chart colors** You can change the color scheme that Excel applies to the chart data markers.

- **Applying a chart style** Excel offers a number of predefined styles that control the chart's colors and effects.
- **Changing the chart data** You can switch the rows and columns, and you can change the PivotTable data source.
- **Changing the chart type** You can change the current chart type to any type that supports PivotCharts.
- **Moving the chart** You can move the PivotChart to a new sheet, or you can embed the PivotChart in a different worksheet.

To change the row, column, or filter options in a PivotChart

→ Click either the row field, column field, or report field button, and then select the options you want to apply to the PivotChart.

To apply styles to a PivotChart

1. Select the PivotChart.

2. On the **Design** tab, do any of the following:

   - In the **Chart Layouts** group, in the **Add Chart Elements** list, add one or more elements to the PivotChart.
   - In the **Chart Layouts** group, in the **Add Quick Layout** list, apply a predefined chart layout.
   - In the **Chart Styles** group, in the **Chart Styles** gallery, apply a predefined style to the PivotChart.
   - In the **Data** group, click **Switch Row/Column** to switch the PivotChart's row and column fields.
   - In the **Data** group, click **Select Data** to choose a different PivotTable as the PivotChart's data source.
   - In the **Type** group, click **Change Chart Type** to apply a new chart type to the PivotChart.
   - In the **Location** group, click **Move Chart** to move the PivotChart either to a new sheet or to an existing worksheet, as an embedded object.

Drill down into PivotChart details

By definition, both a PivotTable and a PivotChart are summaries of the underlying data. This means that each data point is the highest level in a hierarchy that can include many different levels. For example, you might have a PivotChart that summarizes invoice data by showing the total quantity sold for each product category. The category is the highest level of the hierarchy. One level down in the hierarchy might be the individual products that make up each category. An example of a multilevel hierarchy would be to break down the categories into the countries/regions in which the sales occurred, then the states/provinces, and then the cities.

You use the Show Detail dialog box to select the next level of the hierarchy you want to see for the selected data point. In the PivotChart, Excel expands the data point to show its underlying detail. Excel also offers the Collapse command, which you can use to move up the hierarchy to display fewer details.

In a PivotChart, you can use the Show Detail dialog box to drill down into a data field value's details.

To drill down into a PivotChart's details

1. Right-click the data point you want to drill down into.

2. Click **Expand/Collapse**, and then click **Expand** to open the Show Detail dialog box.

3. Click the detail field you want to see, and then click **OK**.

To collapse a PivotChart's details

1. Right-click the data point you want to collapse, and then click **Expand/Collapse**.

2. Do one of the following:

   - Click **Collapse** to collapse a single level.
   - Click **Collapse Entire Field** to collapse all the details and see only the top level of the hierarchy.
   - Click **Collapse to "*Field*"** to collapse all the details up to the field name specified by *Field*.

Objective 4.3 practice tasks

The practice file for these tasks is located in the **MOSExcelExpert2016 \Objective4** practice file folder. The folder also contains a result file that you can use to check your work.

➤ Open the **ExcelExpert_4-3** workbook and do the following:

❑ From the PivotTable on the **Sales by Weekday** worksheet, create a PivotChart of the default type on a new chart sheet. Rename the chart sheet <u>Sales PivotChart</u>.

❑ From the PivotTable on the **Shippers by Location** worksheet, create a clustered column PivotChart and embed it on the same worksheet.

➤ From the table on the **Invoices** worksheet, create a PivotTable and embedded PivotChart on a new worksheet, and do the following:

❑ Rename the worksheet <u>Quantity Sold</u>.

❑ Set up the PivotTable to summarize the Quantity sold by Country/ Region (row) and Category (column).

❑ To the PivotChart, add the chart title <u>Quantity Sold by Category and Country/Region</u>.

❑ In the PivotChart, select the data point where the Country/Region is *United States* and the Category is *Seafood*, and then expand this data point to drill down to the *State/Province* field.

➤ Save the workbook.

➤ Open the **ExcelExpert_4-3_results** workbook. Compare the two workbooks to check your work. Then close the open workbooks.

Index

About the author

PAUL McFEDRIES is a Microsoft Excel expert and full-time technical writer. Paul has been authoring computer books since 1991 and has more than 90 books to his credit, which combined have sold more than 4 million copies worldwide. His titles include the Que Publishing books *Formulas and Functions for Microsoft Excel 2016*, *My Office 2016*, *Windows 10 In Depth* (with coauthor Brian Knittel), and *PCs for Grownups*, in addition to the Wiley Publishing books *Excel Data Analysis* and *Excel PivotTables and PivotCharts Visual Blueprint*. Paul is also the proprietor of Word Spy (*www.wordspy.com*), a website devoted to *lexpionage*, the sleuthing of new words and phrases that have entered the English language. Please drop by Paul's personal website at *www.mcfedries.com* or follow Paul on Twitter, at *twitter.com/paulmcf* and *twitter.com/wordspy*.

Now that you've read the book...

Tell us what you think!

Was it useful?
Did it teach you what you wanted to learn?
Was there room for improvement?

Let us know at https://aka.ms/tellpress

Your feedback goes directly to the staff at Microsoft Press,
and we read every one of your responses. Thanks in advance!